Praise for *Choosing Hope*

"Stranded on an island of unfathomable tragedy and profound despair in the days after she and her students survived the horror of the Sandy Hook murders, first grade teacher Kaitlin Roig-DeBellis looked longingly at life proceeding on the mainland of normalcy. *Choosing Hope* is her moving account of how she returned to that mainland by promoting generosity and accessing faith and positive thinking. Readers who themselves are grieving may find comfort in Roig-DeBellis's story and her design for moving forward."

—Wally Lamb, *New York Times*–bestselling author of
We Are Water and *She's Come Undone*

"A brave book by a courageous woman that reveals the healing power of compassion."

—Karen Armstrong, *New York Times*–bestselling author of *Twelve Steps to a Compassionate Life* and *A History of God*

"In *Choosing Hope*, Kaitlin Roig-DeBellis shows what being tough, courageous, and compassionate is all about. In the face of unspeakable tragedy and horror, she gives us a beautiful portrait of the power of hope and love in the healing of a person, a community, and a country."

—Gabrielle Giffords, former congresswoman and
New York Times–bestselling author

"Intensely moving."   —*New York Daily News*

"Roig-DeBellis, a brave teacher who saved her kids, reveals one of the least known and most bewildering stories from the aftermath of the Sandy Hook Elementary School massacre. When she asked for a few common-sense accommodations for her traumatized first-graders—such as a better door and a ladder out a window—she was told to stop asking. She didn't. Finally faced with the choice of continuing to advocate for her students' safety and peace of mind, or keeping quiet to be able to stay in her classroom, she decided she couldn't be silent about what mattered most and had to leave. So she found a way to help all students nationwide with a new approach to teaching kindness. It is a book that parents and teachers will connect with deeply."

—Jay Mathews, education columnist, *Washington Post*, and bestselling author of *Work Hard. Be Nice.*

"For anyone who has despaired at the human condition, at the horrors we perpetrate onto each other, Kaitlin Roig-DeBellis tells a story that shares our heartbreak and then, just as persuasively, offers us the only possible way forward."

—Amanda Ripley, *New York Times*–bestselling author of *The Smartest Kids in the World* and *The Unthinkable*

"A beautifully written book that demonstrates the power of the human spirit."

—Adam Braun, *New York Times*–bestselling author of *The Promise of a Pencil*

"*Choosing Hope* is part memoir, part testimonial, and all heart. Ms. Roig-DeBellis witnessed the absolute worst of mankind and survived; in its aftermath, she chose to move forward—and she implores readers to do the same, regardless of their circumstances. By choosing hope over pessimism, love over hate, and compassion over ambivalence, we choose to live within light even when darkness threatens to descend. That's a lesson entirely worthy of learning, and sharing—and there's nobody better to teach it." —Examiner.com

"Every day teachers go beyond the call of duty, touching children's lives. . . . Kaitlin is proof of that in so many ways."
—Otha Thornton, president of National PTA

"What a fantastic, straightforward and authentic book. In *Choosing Hope*, Kaitlin Roig-DeBellis exemplifies the power of the five dimensions of crisis leadership by successfully confronting the critical questions that have long concerned those of us in the field . . . such as controlling how deep into the emotional basement we fall and also how to ascend out of it. But all readers—especially teachers, parents and those in emergency professions—will find much to stimulate their thinking in this book, which contains everything anyone needs to know about overcoming trauma. I'll be recommending it to all of my colleagues."
—Professor Isaac Ashkenazi, International Expert for Crisis Management & Leadership, Ben Gurion University of the Negev

"*Choosing Hope* is an inspiring story of a young teacher's triumph over the unimaginable tragedy of the Sandy Hook school massacre. It is also a cautionary tale about school administrators who don't listen. There are many more Kaitlins in our classrooms than we know. We must cherish them."

—Tony Wagner, bestselling author of *The Global Achievement Gap* and *Creating Innovators*

"*Choosing Hope* is a stirring memoir, capturing not only the brutality of the Sandy Hook tragedy but the incredible heroism, resilience, and grace that emerged in its wake. Kaitlin Roig-DeBellis's deep love for her students makes this a bold, inspiring, and ultimately hopeful book."

—Arianna Huffington, cofounder and editor-in-chief of the *Huffington Post* and author of the *New York Times* bestseller *Thrive*

"Teachers rescue children every day by teaching them the skills they need to succeed in life. But no teacher expects to have to rescue her students from a deadly attack. Kaitlin Roig-DeBellis's quick thinking and swift action saved her students' lives. In her book *Choosing Hope*, Kaitlin honors the memory of the children and educators whose lives were lost on that sad day."

—Laura Bush, former First Lady of the United States

Choosing
HOPE

HOW I MOVED FORWARD

from

LIFE'S DARKEST HOUR

KAITLIN ROIG-DEBELLIS

with Robin Gaby Fisher

G. P. PUTNAM'S SONS

New York

G. P. Putnam's Sons
Publishers Since 1838
An imprint of Penguin Random House LLC
375 Hudson Street
New York, New York 10014

Scripture quotation on page 67 taken from the Good News Translation in
Today's English Version, second edition © 1992 by the American Bible Society.

Scripture quotation on pages 124–125 taken from the ESV Bible (The Holy Bible,
Englsih Standard Version) © 2001 by Crossway, a publishing ministry of
Good News Publishers. All rights reserved.

The Paradoxical Commandments are reprinted with the permission
of the author © Kent M. Keith 1969, renewed 2001.

The Library of Congress has catalogued the G. P. Putnam's Sons
hardcover edition as follows:

Roig-DeBellis, Kaitlin.
Choosing hope : moving forward from life's darkest hours / Kaitlin Roig-DeBellis with
Robin Gaby Fisher.
p.   cm.
ISBN 9780399174452
1. Sandy Hook Elementary School Massacre, Newtown, Conn., 2012.   2. School
shootings—Connecticut—Newtown.   3. Mental healing.   4. Psychic trauma.
5. Roig-DeBellis, Kaitlin.   6. Teachers—Connecticut—Newtown—Biography.
I. Fisher, Robin Gaby.   II. Title.
LB3013.33.C8R64   2015   2015015834
371.7'82097469—dc23

First G. P. Putnam's Sons hardcover edition / October 2015
First G. P. Putnam's Sons trade paperback edition / October 2016
G. P. Putnam's Sons trade paperback ISBN: 9780425282311

Printed in the United States of America
1   3   5   7   9   10   8   6   4   2

Book design by Meighan Cavanaugh

This book is dedicated to anyone who ever has gone, ever will go, or is now going through their own darkest hour and to those who helped me through mine.

I am eternally grateful to each of you.

"All glory comes from daring to begin."

—EUGENE F. WARE, from the
poem "John Brown"

CONTENTS

MY DARKEST HOUR

CHOOSING TO OVERCOME

CHOOSING YOUR PATH

CHOOSING HOPE

October 2014

To my Sixteen Fantastic Friends,

    *This is the way we began each day, in a letter from
me to you. The letter always explained, in detail, what
we would do that day. It seemed the only appropriate way
to begin this book, with a letter to you, to explain exactly
why I wrote it.*

    *Above all else, I was inspired to write it for you. I
wrote it because we've already had to endure our darkest
hour (one I wish we hadn't) and I want to inspire anyone
else who is going through a difficult time to know that
they can walk through their pain and come out on the
other side, like we did.*

    *I wrote it because I want you to know that the choice
of how to react to whatever happens in your life is yours
alone to make and I hope that, no matter how challenging
things may seem, you can always choose hope.*

    *Although our school year ended more than a year ago,
and you are no longer my first-graders, I will always
think of you as my students. I will remember how you
were each filled with enthusiasm, excitement, and passion*

for every lesson. I will remember your endless energy. It was contagious. I will remember your twinkling eyes and the happy spell they cast over me. I will remember how you were helpful and hardworking and kind. And I will always remember how brave and strong each of you was in the face of such horror.

The theme of this book is choice. In your lives, you hold the power to make your own good choices. I wish for you that you choose your purpose, know it, follow it, and work hard at it. I wish for you that you choose a positive perspective on how you view the world around you (no matter what happens), and that you always stay open to the opportunities life will present. I wish for you that you are always able to overcome the hard times. And I wish that, no matter how hopeless something may seem, you always decide to choose hope.

I am forever proud of every one of you, and eternally grateful for the honor of being your teacher.

Love,
Miss Roig

Choosing

HOPE

PROLOGUE

"It's no use going back to yesterday, because I was a different person then."

—ALICE, TO THE CHESHIRE CAT, IN LEWIS CARROLL'S *Alice's Adventures in Wonderland*

I live every day wishing I could go back to December 13, back to who I was, who my kids were, back to our school with those who were taken on that day and the life I would never in a million years have changed.

Sometimes I wonder how all of this happened. How, after finding myself in the midst of such abject darkness, in a place where breaking free seemed unlikely, if not impossible, I was finally able to get to the light. Did my strong faith play a role in my passage from that unimaginable tragedy? Yes, it did. Did the love of my family and friends and the support of a caring community bolster me as I attempted to put one foot in front of the other in the days and weeks afterward? Of course. But what saved me, when I dropped to my lowest point and wandered aimlessly between feelings of sadness and fear and maddening frustration over not being able to answer the "Why?" of what happened, was the moment I realized I had a choice. I could allow the actions of a monster to crush my spirit and, for the rest of my life, have that terrible day in Newtown define me. Or I could decide that, even in the wake of such unspeakable malice, I could live a purposeful life by choosing hope.

The Sandy Hook Elementary School massacre was the worst mass murder of schoolchildren in the United States since the Bath School bombing in 1927, and a mournful chapter in our country's narrative. I'll leave it to others to write the historical account of that day. I'll tell my story, but on my terms. I will not be exploitative: anyone who is looking for that should reach for a different book. I will bear witness to the trauma my students and I suffered, and, even more significantly, the acts of heroism that day, and the generosity of others that poured into our broken community afterward. I leave it to readers to decide whether they even want to read, in the section titled "My Darkest Hour," about what we endured. You need not read those particular pages in order to capture the message of hope that I intend to convey with this book. I write about my personal experience for the purpose of clarity and perspective. It is that which led me to the path I walk today.

Six of my colleagues and twenty first-graders—six- and seven-year-olds who were still learning to tell time, and count to 120, and spell 100 words—were murdered that morning. Teachers and administrators and support staff and children who acted with great courage in the face of death. By the grace of God, my students and I survived. When the shooting began and the killer stalked down the hallway toward our classroom, leaving a trail of devastation in his wake, I stuffed my frantic students into a first-grade bathroom that was too tiny for one adult and told them to stay perfectly quiet. I was certain we were going to die.

I won't say the shooter's name. I never have. The only names that need to be memorialized are the innocent children and educators whose lives he took. To this day, I believe the killer came into our classroom, which was the first one in the hallway, and, thinking it was empty, moved to the next classroom, and the next, shooting everyone he saw. I'll never know for sure.

When you hear the whisper of death, life takes on a different meaning. Not a moment passes when I don't recognize that it could have been us who didn't make it out of the school that day. That all of my students and I did get out alive is, in my mind, nothing short of a miracle. I honor that miracle by not taking anything for granted. Not a beautiful sunset, or the gentle sensation of a loved one's hand reaching for mine, or the sweet sound of a child's voice, or a kind word from a stranger. Not for a second.

Because we survived, I must live up to my responsibility to those who were silenced by using my voice to share what I have learned from standing at the precipice of death and, in doing so, making sure that day is not forgotten. Had it been my kids and me who were taken, I would have wanted someone to use his or her voice for good and to carry on the legacy of love and benevolence that, before evil visited, was the story of Sandy Hook.

In the weeks after the shooting, I waded through my sorrow, wondering if I would ever feel joy again. I spent every day asking myself, *Why our school? Why innocent children?* When the answers wouldn't come, I became increasingly frustrated and angry. Until, one day, I realized I would never answer those questions and I needed to concentrate on the ones I could answer, for the sake of both my students and me. Only then could we begin healing. Two questions guided me: How do I make sure that the deeds of a madman do not prevent us from moving forward to live good and meaningful lives? And how do we gain back the sense of control that he took from us? Those two questions led me in everything

I did. Rather than consuming myself with the horror of what happened, I began focusing on the good that could be done, and how I might take part in our collective healing.

When I changed my thinking, I was able to see opportunities. I founded a nonprofit called Classes 4 Classes, a concept to teach students everywhere the importance of kindness and caring for others. In my capacity as a survivor, I was asked to speak to a group of educators, which I reluctantly accepted. I started my presentation by sharing my story of hope and saw the impact it had on the audience. One speaking engagement led to dozens. Following every appearance, people came up to me to share their personal struggles—"I was just diagnosed with cancer"; "I lost my husband"; "My son is going through a difficult time"—and to thank me for inspiring them to focus on the possibilities rather than the negativity in their lives. They would often begin by saying things such as "I know this is nothing like what you've been through" or "My struggle can't compare with yours," and I would stop them each time and say, "Pain is pain and sadness is sadness and loss is loss and we are all connected in this."

After a few of these encounters, I decided that if, by sharing my personal story, I could help even one person through his or her darkest hour, then that was what I needed to do. I quickly realized that helping them was healing me. Sharing my message of hope became my calling. So when I was approached about writing a book, something that had never crossed my mind, I decided to seize the opportunity to be able to reach even more people.

The Sandy Hook Elementary School I knew closed its doors for good after the shooting. Our beautiful school is dust now, razed to the soil because what it came to represent was too painful for a community to bear. And while teaching is at the core of who I am, my new classroom is wherever life takes me—to elementary schools, and teacher conferences, and college commencements, and anywhere else I am asked to speak.

In my travels and, now, with my book, my purpose is to convey the importance of gratitude and endurance and, most of all, the power of choice. Yes, especially that. I know now that how you deal with life's challenges, even those that may seem unbearable or hopeless, is your choice to make. Bad things happen to all of us, things that test us and impact us and change us, but it is not those moments that define who we are. It is how we choose to react to them that does. You can give in and give up or you can decide to live your life with intent and love and compassion for others and for yourself. You can choose hope, even in the darkest hour, and in that choice you will find light. We have that power. I do. You do. Everyone does. That is what I believe.

Ever since I was a little girl and my mom introduced me to Robert Frost, I have loved the poem "The Road Not Taken." In that poem, Frost famously wrote,

> *I shall be telling this with a sigh*
> *Somewhere ages and ages hence:*
> *Two roads diverged in a wood, and I—*
> *I took the one less traveled by,*
> *And that has made all the difference.*

When I reached a crossroads in my journey back from that terrible day in 2012, I chose hope. And that has made all the difference.

My name is Kaitlin Roig-DeBellis and this is my story.

CHOOSING

YOUR PURPOSE

"The meaning of life is to find your gift. The purpose
of life is to give it away."

—Pablo Picasso

2012

It might sound like a cliché, but Sandy Hook Elementary School was a special place. When you walked through the front doors, you could just feel the love inside. It started at the top with our principal, a spirited, vivacious woman with a huge heart, and filtered down to the staff and the students. We just didn't have bad days at Sandy Hook. It was always sunny inside. My teaching career began there, and I can honestly say that if someone had offered me another job for three times the salary, I would have turned it down.

I started the 2012 school year with the same anticipation and excitement I had on my first day of teaching there, six years earlier. Sixteen new little rosy faces. Clean slates. Six- and seven-year-olds who were happy to be in school and keen to learn. I was eager to grow with my new class. Teachers know that our personal growth is what makes us effective in the classroom, so I'd always tried to gain as much experience as I could pack into my schedule. I knew I was a good teacher, but I always aimed to be better. That year, I'd signed on for the committee for language arts, which focused on instituting a new reading program for our students. When I wasn't doing that, I was helping to refine the first-grade curriculum, or studying new and innovative teaching skills, or coaching students for Marathon Mondays, a running club for third- and fourth-graders, many of them former students of mine who knew about my passion for long-distance running. But my favorite thing was being in the classroom with my first-graders. For me, it was occupational bliss.

My personal life had also taken a happy turn at about that time. Two weeks before school started, my boyfriend proposed to me. I'd never been that girl who went wedding-dress shopping before she ever met her future husband, but I did know I wanted to be married and have my own children someday. I'd met Nick, by chance, three years earlier and knew right away that he was the one. Our first meeting was, in so many ways, a fluke. Or was it fate? I'd like to think so.

It was August 18, 2009. I'd planned to meet my former college roommate and one of my best friends, Lisa, for dinner on that Tuesday to talk about training together for the Boston Half Marathon. As it happened, the restaurant we chose was closed on Tuesdays, so Lisa and I had settled on a place nearby called John's cafe. I'd reserved a table for two outside, for 6:30, I thought. Lisa thought the reservation was for 6:00. When I got there, thirty minutes after she did, I found Lisa sitting at the bar, sipping a glass of wine and chatting up the bartender. I didn't know it then, but Lisa had told the bartender how to spot me. "She's blond, she always smiles, and she'll say 'Hey!' as if she isn't late," she'd said.

"Hey!" I said, smiling my best smile as I strolled in and joined her at the bar. "Hey!" Lisa said. "Kaitlin, meet Nick. Nick, this is Kaitlin." I soon learned that Nick's brother was the chef at John's. Nick was between jobs as a country-club superintendent and bartending there, but only on Tuesday nights. He poured me a glass of wine and the three of us started talking about, well, just stuff. I told him I'd graduated from the University of Connecticut. He'd graduated from Rutgers. He coached football and played golf. I like long runs and spending time with my family and friends. We discovered our hometowns were only ten minutes apart and we had some mutual acquaintances. Talking with Nick was so natural, so easy. By the end of the evening, we were Facebook friends.

———

The next morning I found a Facebook message from Nick saying how much he'd enjoyed our time together and asking if I'd like to have lunch the following week. I didn't hesitate with my response. "Of course!" I wrote. Nick and I shared everything after that. We traveled to Miami every August and December. We celebrated Thanksgivings with his family and Christmases with mine. We took vacations with friends to Cape Cod and Atlantic City. We hiked up mountains, jogged along beaches, cooked each other's favorite meals, ate out at our favorite restaurants, and made each other's friends "our friends." My dad had always told me that when it came time for me to choose a life partner, it should be someone who treasured me (the way he has always treasured my mom), and I had found that in Nick. Three years to the day after that first meeting, he proposed.

Nick is such a romantic that a simple "Will you marry me?" wouldn't do. He'd put a lot of thought into how he would ask me to marry him. I'd run in from the gym that day and found him sitting on the bed, looking at his iPad. Months earlier, he had compiled a timeline of photos from our courtship and turned it into a slideshow with Journey's "When You Love a Woman"—our song—playing in the background. It was quite a keepsake, with photos of us on early dates, and on vacations, and celebrating the holidays, and birthdays, and other special occasions. We never tired of watching it, so I wasn't surprised to see it on his screen. "I added some photos," Nick said, patting the bed for me to sit down. I was sweaty from working out and just wanted a shower, but Nick insisted I sit, so I did, admittedly a little bit annoyed. (That's how it always is, right? I had no idea what was about to come.)

We watched the same slideshow of the same photos I'd seen a million times—until he got to the last picture. It was of a beautiful engagement ring, a gold band with a bright yellow citrine stone in the center. Once I caught my breath, I turned to look at him and he was already down on one knee. "I've been waiting a long time to do this and I know you've been waiting, too," he said. "Will you marry me?" In anticipation of my response (a tearful "Yes!") Nick had invited our closest friends for a celebratory brunch at our place that same afternoon, which he prepared himself. My parents were thrilled when I called to tell them we were engaged. In a wonderful gesture, a few weeks earlier, Nick had taken my dad to play golf and, unbeknownst to me, asked for his permission to marry me. He's old-fashioned that way, and so is my dad.

That same day we decided that the wedding would take place the following August. The sixteenth, a Friday. Even though it was a year away, I began planning immediately. Within a month, I was headed to New York City with my mom and my best friend, Casey, to buy my dress. I had already chosen it from a picture I'd seen in a magazine. An attentive saleswoman who aimed to please greeted us at the Vera Wang bridal shop on Madison Avenue. "What are you looking for?" she asked. "I know exactly what I want," I replied excitedly. "I would like to try on the model called Gemma." Trying to be accommodating, she pulled a half-dozen or so dresses, including the one I'd requested, for me to try on. I slipped on the Gemma first. It was strapless, with a fitted bodice that was wrapped in French tulle, and it flared at the knee with layers and layers of silk organza. I couldn't imagine a more beautiful dress. "Okay! Wrap it up!" I said. I watched as the saleswoman's mouth dropped. I have no doubt it was the quickest sale she had ever made. From there, Mom, Casey, and I went to lunch in the city and toasted the future with champagne. The countdown had begun. I couldn't wait to tell my class.

There isn't much I don't share with my first-graders, and the news of my engagement was no exception. I planned my announcement for Share Day, a time we set aside to talk about something that had happened in our lives—taking a trip to the zoo, or seeing a movie, or visiting a grandparent, things like that. Or, sometimes, on Share Days we'd have themes, such as a favorite thing to do, or a family activ-

and everyone was encouraged to participate.

When it was my turn, I announced to my brand-new
first-grade class that I was engaged. During questions and
comments, one of my little boys, who, no matter what we
were discussing, was always curious for clarification, raised
his hand right up.

"Miss Roig?" he asked, pushing fringes of hair away from
inquisitive eyes. "Does *engaged* mean you're getting married
or you're getting divorced?"

I couldn't help but smile. "Oh!" I said. "*Engaged* means
you're going to be married."

The boy took a deep breath and blew it out. "Whew!" he
said. "I was worried there for a minute."

And so the school year began, as sweet and enchanting as
ever. How could I not love what I was doing?

First Grade Is . . .

Learning the difference between tattling and telling.
Being excited about every little thing, because everything is new.

17

Going to the bathroom several times a day.

Three and three-quarters inches, fifty pounds, gap-toothed smiles.

Wanting to help, with everything.

Asking questions. Who? What? When? Where? How? Why? Why? Why?

All about routines. (Pity the poor substitute teacher: "That's not how Miss Roig does it! That's not where we put that! That's not the right way . . .)

Having no filter. The truth is the truth is the truth. ("You look so tired!" "You look beautiful!" "Why are you wearing those silly shoes?")

Being impulsive. (They do what they want, when they want.)

Runny noses, untied shoes, constant reminders to "Cover your mouth when you sneeze."

Learning how to be a friend.

Learning to say "I'm sorry."

Learning that your actions after you've said "I'm sorry" are what really count.

Learning to tie your shoes.

Talking about "those baby kindergartners."

Not having naptime anymore (even though they could use it!).

Repeating everything you hear (including arguments between your parents!).

Having boundless energy. Going. Going. Going.

Learning to sit for longer periods of time.

Exploring. What can I get away with? What won't work?

Learning to tell time, to count to 120, to spell 100 words, to write a complete sentence.

Seeing things as right or wrong, good or bad, with no middle ground.

Learning to walk in the hallway. ("Voices off!")

Having to be told to "Keep your hands to yourself." Regularly.

Learning about personal space and staying inside of it (crisscross applesauce, hands in a bowl).

Celebrating every holiday, including the one hundredth day of school.

Believing your parents and your teachers are real-life heroes.

It's a magical time for children, and for their teachers. It really is a year of "firsts." The first weeks of school are for students to get familiar with the lay of the land. It's their first time spending the whole day at school (and learning how not to take an afternoon nap the way they did in kindergarten) and it takes some time to get them used to the routine. I always took my students on "guided discovery" trips, to places like the cafeteria, where they could explore the offerings, and outside to the playground, where I demonstrated how to use the slide, the swings, and the climbing bars.

Back in the classroom, I showed them things such as how to hang up their backpacks, and where to find their book bins, and the process for signing up for the cafeteria lunch. (I learned an important lesson about that during my first year of teaching. The entire class signed up for the school lunch, but when we got to the cafeteria, where the food had already been prepared and waiting for us, I discovered that most of my first-graders weren't buying at all. They had brought their lunches from home. They had just been so excited for an opportunity to sign up for something—how grown-up!—that they all signed up. Needless to say, the lunch ladies were not happy.)

Watching my students experience so many firsts never got old. Those first weeks were, as always, wonderful (and tiring) times. The kids reveled in things such as learning to spell three- and four-letter words, and reading the face on a clock to the nearest hour, and remembering one another's names, and memorizing the classroom rules:

1. Take care of everything in our class and our school.
2. Take care of myself.
3. Show other people respect.
4. Always try my best.

We were really starting to come together as a class.

But September became October, and that rolled into November, and then December 14, when everything came to a numbing halt.

For my students and me that day began like most days. I had just finished playing a recording of "Oh, What a Beautiful Mornin'," the Rogers and Hammerstein classic from the musical *Oklahoma!*, and the cue for my first-graders to gather at the front of our classroom for our morning meeting. Morning meeting was one of my favorite customs, fifteen or twenty minutes at the beginning of class time when we acknowledged one another with a special greeting and got to know and care about one another. It was a great reinforcement for our number-one classroom rule, the Golden Rule: do unto others as you would want them to do unto you.

When I allow my mind to drift back to that memory, I imagine us as a Norman Rockwell painting. There we are, Miss Roig and her fifteen little pumpkins, giggly girls with freckled noses and ponytails tied with bows, and squirmy boys with cowlicks and scraped-up knees, all sitting "criss-cross applesauce, hands in the bowl" in a circle in a cozy corner of our classroom.

I wish I could have frozen that snapshot in time, those precious moments of us, a young teacher and her class of first-graders—little boys and girls whose biggest worries were what their moms had packed for lunch, or what Santa was bringing for Christmas, or when a loose tooth was finally going to come out—that sweet morning time just before a twenty-year-old local man, cloaked all in black, and carrying a Bushmaster semiautomatic rifle, blasted his way into our school and went on a killing spree.

One minute, I was deliriously happy, with a career I loved and a man I cherished. The next minute, I was crammed into a bathroom stall with my terror-struck first-graders—boys and girls, most of whom had yet to even learn to tie their shoes—mourning the future we would never have and listening in horror as the teachers and first-graders on the other side of the wall were being massacred, the whole time thinking that we were next. I could hardly grasp what was happening. It couldn't be. Not to us. Not in Newtown. But that's how life is, isn't it? It can change in a blink.

When I finally got home on that mournful afternoon, dazed by the madness of what I had witnessed, thinking about the children and educators who had lost their lives so senselessly and cruelly, I couldn't imagine my students or me ever knowing "normal" again, ever feeling true happiness or joy after knowing such maliciousness and evil. How does a child recapture that wondrous view of the world they had when they've witnessed the very worst of humankind?

I was so angry for them and for me that my tears tasted of bitterness and my hands balled up into tight fists. The monster had taken our friends, ripped away our ideals, shaken our faith in humanity, and blunted our optimism. I was overcome with feelings of resentment and loathing. The stranger had destroyed the fairy tale. Still, I prayed for my students and for me that one day we would find a reason to smile again.

I hoped I could figure out how.

The Common Denominator

Acouple years back I read a column in *The New York Times* about a first-grade boy who was struggling in school. His home life was turbulent and his schoolwork suffered so much that he was eventually placed in a class for slow learners. The boy decided that if his teachers had such low expectations of him he might as well "live down" to those ambitions. In fourth grade, he moved to a different school district. His new teacher cared enough to engage and encourage him, and—what do you know?—he began to enjoy learning. Lo and behold, that young boy wasn't "slow" at all. On the contrary, his IQ was so high he was eventually placed in a gifted and talented program and went on to become valedictorian of his high school graduating class.

Charles Blow, the *Times* columnist, was that little boy.

Reading about how a teacher named Mrs. Harris changed his path really hit home for me. I can't help but wonder how different Mr. Blow's life might be had he never gotten the opportunity to work with a teacher who cared enough to believe in him. What a huge responsibility we, as teachers, have to inspire and encourage, and what a tremendous impression we can make on our students' lives when we do our jobs the right way.

Our job is to encourage our students, to believe in them and inspire them to want to learn and be the best they can be. That is what good teachers do. They light a fire under their students with the goal of leading them to be intrinsic, lifelong learners. Learners who can find knowledge on their own, explore, inquire, and still have a yearning to know more.

During my years in the classroom, I witnessed countless stories of teachers who identified the hidden promise of students and worked tirelessly to instigate learning to help them reach their potential. Teachers are often maligned, and I know there are some out there who should probably be in different professions, but in my experience, most are wholly devoted, caring, competent people with the altruistic goal of sharing their knowledge to engage children in learning. I can think of no nobler cause.

Someone recently asked me, "What would the world be

like without teachers?" Without hesitation, I replied, "It wouldn't work." Teachers are why the world works. I have always believed that. They're the common denominator in our world. Everyone starts in school—doctors, lawyers, athletes, business moguls, cancer researchers, and presidents. Think about Anne Sullivan, the "miracle worker" who devoted her entire adult life to helping Helen Keller become an intellectually productive human being. The thing about teachers, the really good ones, is that their passion for what they do awakens young minds to the joys of learning, and after that, anything is possible.

Good teachers plant seeds and help to cultivate good and thoughtful people.

It's not enough to make an impression on one or two of your students. You strive to instill self-confidence and a love of learning in every student, but you have to love what you're doing to want to put in the time and effort it takes to accomplish that. It's kind of like an actor who performs for the same audience every day and still has them wanting to come back for more. That kind of passion is contagious and the audience catches it.

Some of the most influential people in the history of the world were teachers. Think about it. Confucius. Aristotle. Albert Einstein. Henry David Thoreau. Booker T. Washington. They shaped minds and cultures. Barack Obama famously said during his first run for president in 2008, "The single most important factor in determining [student] achievement is not the color of their skin or where they come from. It's not who their parents are or how much money they have. It's who their teacher is." I couldn't agree more.

A good teacher wears many hats: educator, supporter, nurse, counselor, mediator, listener, sometimes even parent. You intervene when your students aren't seeing eye to eye. You encourage confidence in those who may be struggling with self-image. You build a caring community within your classroom so that everyone feels as if they are part of the team.

Most of the teachers I know have willingly stepped into these custodial roles. I've watched my peers bring timid students out of their shells enough to be able to make new friends, and give introverted students the confidence to take a risk and speak in front of their classmates, and convert students who were faltering in their schoolwork into students who loved coming to class.

I watched a teacher work with a young boy with selective mutism, a severe anxiety disorder in which he froze up in class and couldn't speak. Little by little, she got him to open up, and he eventually not only raised his hand in class, he sometimes even initiated conversations. I've known teachers

who've bought their students warm coats and hot meals. I've
known them to work late hours trying to come up with original ways to engage individual students who are difficult to
reach. I've seen cases in which a child who came into school
unable to read even a simple CVC (a consonant, vowel, consonant word, such as *cat*) was reading chapter books by the
end of the year, because the teacher cared enough to put the
extra time in.

The good teacher's job is never really finished. When the
afternoon school bell rings, there's inevitably a student you
take home with you, at least figuratively speaking. The child
who you worry isn't getting enough love at home, or enough
to eat, or who comes to school in the dead of January wearing only a sweatshirt. You don't get evenings and weekends
off from those children. You don't stop thinking about them
at 3:00 on weekdays. You carry them with you as if they
were your own.

Caretaker may not be part of the job description, but good
teachers go where their hearts take them. We become that
kind of teacher because we want that kind of responsibility.
Teaching isn't a job. It's a calling. It doesn't end when the
school day does. We want to be role models for our students,
positive influences, adults they can look up to, a difference-
maker in their lives. The joy of the job is in the giving, and
there is no bigger joy than watching your students grow into

independent learners and thinkers who are also kind, caring, and empathetic people.

What you give to your students comes back tenfold. There is no greater gift than the moment when a student struggling with how to spell a tricky word or how to tell the hour and the half-hour on a clock finally gets it. A hand-made thank-you card or a bunch of freshly picked daisies (with their mother's permission, you hope) from a grateful student is icing on the cake. Then there are those keepsakes they give you at the end of the school year that make saying good-bye a little more bearable, thoughtful little gifts to remember them by, such as signed beach bags and finger-print plates and letters and framed photos of themselves. As if you could forget. I still have every one of the mementos.

I love this quote by Mary Bicouvaris, the 1989 National Teacher of the Year: "When former students return to see me over the years, my heart fills up in the knowledge that I have been part of a wonderful accumulation of experi-ences that followed them through life." I can't imagine any-one saying it better. In what other job do you get to see, every day, the difference you have made in a child's life? How many others get to touch a new set of lives every year? Where else but in a classroom can you impact so many young lives?

Some of my proudest moments have nothing at all to do

with academics, but are those times when you realize your students are just happy to be in your class. I cherish those times when a student has run up to me at the end of the school year and said, "Miss Roig! I want to be a teacher just like you when I grow up!" Or when a student misspeaks and calls you "Mom" because they feel so safe and comforted in your classroom. I have known no warmer feeling than what I've experienced when I'm reminded that I've made a difference in a child's life. I have a box of those reminders tucked away at home. Whenever I need a boost of confidence or my spirits lifted, I take it out and sift through the cards and letters inside from my first-graders over the years. Then all is right with the world.

Dear Miss Roig:

... Thank you for teaching us all the wunderfil things. Self-control, raising our hands, reading our books, walking in line. You are a very nice teacher.
... Thank you for teaching me avrything in first grade you need to know for sekint grade.
... Thank you for teaching me how to read. You are the best teacher ever.
... Thank you for helping me learn about shapes.

. . . You are a nice teacher, and fun, too!

. . . You are the best teacher in the world because you help me when I am stuck doing my writing.

. . . You taught me how to tell time. I love telling time! You made first grade so much fun!

Miss Roig is special because:

. . . she is the best teacher. We do fun things like butterflies, personal narratives, and math tests. I will always remember first grade for the rest of my life!

. . . she is really fun, she reads us good stories and helps us if we get stuck when we are writing. I love school because Miss Roig is my teacher.

. . . is speshal. She teaches us how to read and write. She teaches us about butterfliwes and 3D and 2D shapes. Miss Roig is nice, too.

. . . she is sweet. She lets us do crafts. She is a good teacher. I have learned many things.

. . . she takes care of all the people in our class. Because she is a great teacher.

. . . she loves all of us. She teaches us lots of things we don't know. She is the best teacher. We love you.

. . . she takes good care of us and Humphrey (the

stuffed animal, a hamster, that was the class pet).
She is very fair. She loves all of her students. She
makes teaching fun. She is very funny. I love Miss
Roig.

. . . she makes first grade fun. I liked having Y-O-U
for a teacher.

. . . shehelpsuswithspellingandhanDwritingandevery-
onelovesherincluDingmeandIwillalwaysremember-
missroig.(heart)

. . . she is the best teacher. Ever! Good job Miss Roig!

When I read and reread those sweet letters, those wonderful gestures of appreciation and kindness, that's when I
know I've done a good job.

Mrs. Beaulier

Everyone, if they are fortunate enough, has had a special teacher growing up. Mine was Mrs. Beaulier in the fifth grade. I'm pretty sure she doesn't know it, but she was the model for the teacher that I ultimately became. I couldn't wait to get to her class every day. Mrs. Beaulier was bubbly and full of life. She was tall, with short brown hair and tan skin, and had the kind of smile that warmed you from the inside. She read us great literature and provoked lively discussions, but she didn't just teach us subjects, things such as multiplying fractions and writing stories and identifying planets in the solar system. She inspired us with her own thirst for knowledge and her eagerness for us to learn, and she had special ways of rewarding us for our efforts, unique ways that were designed to be great motivators.

We had a reading contest called Book It!, for instance. Every time we finished a book we pinned it on a bulletin board in the classroom. When we'd reached a milestone by reading a prescribed number of books, Mrs. Beaulier rewarded us with a special sticker. But the best part was, with each milestone, we also got our own personal pan pizza from Pizza Hut. That was a great motivator for me!

For me, there was only one Mrs. Beaulier. She didn't just *teach*. She was *a teacher*. That was her calling. She put thought into everything she did. Her teaching know-how was matched only by her enthusiasm for getting to know us. She had this way of making everyone in her classroom feel so welcome, and she encouraged us to take an interest in one another as well.

Fifth grade is such a pivotal year, the time when students are transitioning from elementary school to middle school. It's the bridge between being a child and becoming a young adult. Everything is about to change—allegiances, best friends, the place you've gone to school since you were in kindergarten.

For a fifth-grader, leaving the security of the place you've known your whole life for a big, daunting new school with a hierarchy and lockers is frightening and unsettling. Mrs. Beaulier prepared us well for the road ahead. She gave us exercises to help build our confidence before the big, bad seventh- and eighth-graders got their chance at us, as the lowly sixth-graders.

I'll always remember one of the first homework assignments for her class. Our task was to take a box and fill it with things that illustrated who we were. It was our "self-esteem box," a place where we put things we felt really good about. I was so excited. I had never had a teacher who took such a personal interest in me. The purpose of the box was really a way for all of us to introduce ourselves and start to get to know one another. We had a week to put it together before we shared it with the class. I began with a large shoebox and decorated the outside of it with stickers of smiley faces and flowers and cutouts of fashions from a magazine. Inside, I tucked ribbons I'd won from running track, and photos of the cousins I was close to, and neighborhood kids, and family vacations my parents and I had taken to Maine and Cape Cod. I was so proud when I presented it to the class. I might as well have been performing onstage at Radio City Music Hall, that's how excited I was. Mrs. Beaulier beamed and, for the rest of the school year, she talked to me about running and asked about my track meets. She made me feel so special, and I'm certain she made each of her students feel the same way.

Mrs. Beaulier was what I call a "difference maker." She was practicing what she loved, doing what she was meant to do, and that was easy to see. She taught me, by example, that following your heart and pursuing your passion will lead you to your purpose in life. You just have to pay attention and trust that you are on the right path. She was so much more than someone who taught lessons from a book. She was a dedicated educator, a counselor, a mentor, and a life guide.

That was the kind of teacher I aimed to be.

My Friends

I called my students "friends." It was something I'd learned when I was in college and working at the day-care center on campus. It was a way of putting everyone at ease and making the classroom feel like a friendly place to be. I'd start out every morning with a welcoming, "Good morning, Fantastic Friends!" My students loved it. "Good morning, Miss Roig!" they'd chirp with their happy little voices.

Teaching first-graders is a gift. Every day is brand new. It's a point in a child's life when they are experiencing things for the first time and every lesson feels like an adventure to them. They're excited to learn and to try new things, and every day is filled with aha! moments. As their teacher, you get to experience all those firsts, too, through their eyes. And the firsts are different with every class.

I often say that first-graders are the way the world should be. They giggle incessantly, love unconditionally, forgive easily, ask a million questions, and say exactly what's on their mind—no matter what it is that's on their mind. If they think it, they say it. Nothing is modified or edited. I once had a student ask if I was eighty years old "like my grandma." I was twenty-six. Another student asked if I had my own kids, and when I said I didn't, he frowned with concern and asked, "Well, why not? Shouldn't you be married by now?" Then there was the little boy who'd apparently overheard me talking about my boyfriend and asked, I should say rather indignantly, "Miss Roig, should you really be living with your boyfriend before marriage? *Humph.* My mom says . . ." That was just the beginning of his lecture.

They're such funny little beings. Tattletales and gossips. No concept of personal space. They think nothing of sprawling out on their neighbor's desk or draping themselves over the teacher's lap. They are strict enforcers of class rules, but they never take responsibility when they break a rule themselves—and they always blame someone else ("I didn't do it!" "He told me to do it!" "It's her fault!"). They are still losing their baby teeth. They frequently trip and stumble and fall out of their chairs because their balance is not yet fully developed. They ask one another the funniest questions: "How come grown-up people can swear and we can't?"

"Is so-and-so your girlfriend?" ("Ewwwwww.") "Is so-and-so your boyfriend?" (Hysterical giggles.) You just can't help but fall in love with them.

Emerson nailed it when he described a child as a "curly, dimpled lunatic." Who wouldn't want to be around that? First-grade philosophy is straight out of a Dr. Seuss book: "Today was good. Today was fun. Tomorrow is another one." Which is why I always got to school early, bright-eyed, full of energy and optimism, and eager to see what the day would bring. That extra hour or so in the morning allowed me time to prepare for class. Goodness knows that once my students got there I wouldn't get a minute for planning lessons, or organizing their reading material, or anything other than them. That's another thing about first-graders. They're charmingly egocentric and demanding of their teacher's attention, every minute of every day.

I always knew when my students walked through the door in the morning. They came in happily chattering and usually greeted me with a guessing game: "Guess what, Miss Roig?" "Guess what the bus driver said?" "Guess what I did yesterday?" "Guess where I'm going after school?" "Guess how much the tooth fairy left me?" (That one was usually accompanied by a big toothless grin!) Once they were settled into their seats, I rarely thought to look at the clock again until they left for the day. When I wasn't teaching, I was busy tying shoes and blowing noses and sanitizing hands and reminding them to "Please, wash your hands . . . Close the door . . . Push in your chair . . . Sign up for lunch" (and I usually had to remind them three, four, and five times). I embraced each new day as a learning experience, not just for my kids, but also for me. I saw each class as an opportunity to grow as a teacher. If a math lesson didn't go as intended, I'd change it for the following day. If my students started to squirm or seem distracted, I reeled them in by stepping up my own enthusiasm for whatever we were learning, either that or we'd take a "sensory break" or practice our yoga poses. Tomorrow was the chance to build on what worked or didn't work today.

And we always had fun doing it.

My Passion, My Purpose

I have always had a love for working with children. When other kids were playing with dolls and dollhouses, or zooming around in plastic cars pretending to be race car drivers, I was setting up my stuffed animals in neat rows in my room in preparation for the day's lesson. Or, when I was lucky enough, I was able to recruit a couple neighborhood friends as my students while I played teacher. My playroom was my classroom, complete with a whiteboard easel, No. 2 pencils sharpened to razor points, and enough mini-notebooks for everyone. I taught my "students" math and reading and writing, and sometimes I borrowed lessons that my own teachers had taught on that day.

By the time I went to college, I had been a mother's helper, a babysitter, a camp counselor, a day-care facilitator, a youth center volunteer, a study hall monitor, and a student tutor. Nothing could deter me from my work. On second thought, let's change the word *work* to *passion*.

Passion is the fuel that drives dreams. I remember reading that Michael Jordan didn't make the varsity basketball team in high school, but his passion for the sport drove him to become the greatest player of all time. A newspaper editor told Walt Disney that he lacked imagination and original ideas. Disney's passion for artistic creation led to an entertainment empire. Oprah was let go from one of her first broadcasting jobs because her employer said she was unsuitable for television news. Her passion for the medium took her to the top of the talk-show industry. None of these celebrities allowed critics or setbacks to interfere with their passion. They believed in their own potential and dared to follow their dreams. I know it took courage and hard work, but the rewards were great. Their passion became their purpose. And by using their purpose, each one of them, in his or her own way, made a positive impact in our world. Who doesn't want to make her life mean something bigger than herself?

Recognizing my passion so early in my life came to define who I would become as an adult. I wanted to mentor children, to help them become the best people they could possibly be. Being a part of the process of helping them grow into fine adults seemed so worthwhile. In fact, I couldn't imagine anything more rewarding than having a hand in shaping young people's lives. From an early age, everything I did brought me one step closer to my goal. Whether I was potty training a two-year-old boy who insisted that his potty be the tree near his driveway (which was on a main road) or coaching a group of first- and second-graders in a dance routine for an end-of-summer skit at camp, I took the task seriously. Meanwhile, with every experience, I was learning how to be the best teacher I could be.

In high school, I signed up for a class in which the students basically ran an on-site day-care program. We had two teachers and both of them urged me to apply to colleges with strong education majors. I was a natural for the profession, they said. One of them insisted that the University of Delaware had the best program and she was adamant I apply there. Well, I did and I didn't get in. I was crushed. I'd had my heart set on that school, but one rejection letter was not going to deter me from pursuing my passion. Three other schools accepted me and I chose the University of Connecticut, the one closest to home.

My goal was to do well in my undergraduate studies and advance to UConn's prestigious Neag School of Education. I knew I had to shine academically to be a serious contender. In my freshman year I joined a sorority, Kappa Kappa

Gamma, whose members were super-studious, and that really lit a fire under me. My sophomore year was all business. I threw myself into my studies and basically lived at the library on campus. To continue gaining practical experience, I worked at the university's day-care center and volunteered as a youth mentor and reading buddy for elementary school students. My hard work and perseverance paid off and I was accepted into Neag's master's program in my junior year. As a senior, I was inducted into the Historical Honor Society and the Neag Honor Society and named a New England Scholar.

If I didn't know then that I wanted to teach little kids, my mind was certainly made up as I pursued my master's degree. Kindergarten through third grade was the best. The students were so sweet and funny and eager to learn. Everything is a lightbulb moment for them. One of my favorite stories is from my final semester, when I was interning at the local grade school. Three of us from the master's program teamed up to help the faculty there implement the concept of High-Order Thinking into their guided reading program for first- through third-graders. High-Order Thinking is a method in which students are asked questions in a way that helps them to dissect and comprehend information and not simply memorize it. Our team project was putting together a small, bound book with focus questions for each area of comprehension. It was interesting work, but I wanted to work with the kids.

I finally got my wish toward the end of the school year when I was assigned to observe a kindergarten class. I was so excited. One day, the teacher asked me to read a book to the students, and they all gathered in a circle around my chair. I don't remember the name of the book anymore, but the theme was diversity and acceptance. The message of the story was that we all have similarities and differences, but we are all special, and differences should be celebrated, not judged. Just as I was finishing reading the last page of the book, one little boy's hand shot up. He was sitting in the front row, so I could hardly miss him. When I didn't respond immediately, he began to shake his raised hand. He was jumping out of his skin. He really wanted to tell me something. I noticed he was holding the arm of one of his classmates, the only African American child in the class. When I finished reading and finally called on him, he was wide-eyed and breathless. "Miss Roig!" he cried. "Miss Roig! This book is just like our class! Ben is black and everyone else is white!" The other little boy looked down at his arm and his mouth dropped. "Oh my God!" he exclaimed. "I am black!" He was absolutely serious. Until then, he had apparently never noticed he was different from the other kids. It was the most wonderful moment, and such a credit to his parents and his teacher.

That's why I wanted to be a teacher. I wanted to be part of that kind of world.

I graduated from the master's program with honors in 2006. I was twenty-one years old. That fall, I took a long-term subbing job as a reading specialist in Westport, Connecticut, and sent my résumé out to every district that had an elementary school with an opening. The Newtown Public School District was one of the districts that responded, requesting that I apply for a position to teach the fourth grade. I wanted to be a first-grade teacher, but I went to the interview anyway.

The principal and I hit if off and the next day she called. "I have bad news and good news," she said. "The bad news is that I hired a teacher who had lots of fourth-grade experience. The good news is a first-grade position has just opened up. Would you like it?"

I felt like jumping up and down (and maybe I did). "Absolutely!" I cried. "First grade is my dream!" I could hardly believe that my lifelong passion was about to become my purpose. I couldn't wait to get started.

CHOOSING YOUR PERSPECTIVE

"We are all in the gutter, but some of us are looking at the stars."

—OSCAR WILDE, *Lady Windemere's Fan*

Kate's Day

The way I see it, my entire life prepared me for the journey I am on today. I have always been a positive person. It's something I hold tightly to, my optimistic outlook on life. I am a glass-half-full kind of person. I smile a lot. I love unabashedly. I feel joy at the slightest things. In many ways, I have the heart of a child, and maybe that's why my first-graders and I relate so well to one another. I don't do cynical well. I figured out a long time ago that there's nothing positive about being negative. I'm not saying there aren't times that I'm angry or sad or disappointed, because everyone has challenges. The mean girls in school bullied me for being too thin. My heart's been broken and I've lost in love. I've grieved the deaths of cherished family members. But I also understand that a rich life means you feel all of the deep emotions, not just the happy ones. Acknowledging anger and sadness and disappointments is the first step in working through the tests that are put in our path. With the good there is bad, and with the bad there is good. That is life. Yet how we look at the day is our choice to make, and I really try to face every encounter by looking for something positive to cling to.

Perspective is such a powerful tool. It determines the quality of our lives. I've known people who seem to have everything, yet they always take the point of view of a pessimist, focusing on what they think they want but don't have. On the other hand, especially since the tragedy, I've met people who are facing wrenching challenges—the death of a child, a terminal illness—and they've chosen to set their eyes on whatever light they can find in the world. Those are the kinds of people I want to be around.

In *Letters from My Garden*, the French novelist wrote, "You complain about seeing thorny rose bushes; Me, I rejoice and give thanks to the gods." Although now I have witnessed the worst of mankind, I have chosen to embrace gratitude as a way of focusing on the abundant good in the world and the inherent kindness of people, because that is just as real. I suppose, especially in light of what happened at our school, I could make the tragedy and all of its crushing implications the focal point of my day-to-day living. I could focus on the truths that terrible things happen to us and malevolence exists in the world, the negative over the positive. In fact, I did for weeks after the shootings. But what does that accomplish?

I think about Stephen Hawking, the renowned physicist who has become progressively disabled with the motor-neuron disease amyotrophic lateral sclerosis (ALS), colloquially called Lou Gehrig's disease. Hawking is confined to a wheelchair and speaks through a computerized speech synthesizer. His disease has no cure and he needs full-time care, yet his perspective is defined by something he said during one of the many interviews he's conducted over the years. "When one's expectations are reduced to zero, one really appreciates everything one does," he is quoted as saying. Maybe that's why he's lived literally decades past doctors' diagnoses that he'd be dead within two and a half years. How easy would it be for him to get stuck in the negative and be bitter over what has been taken from him? And how would that impact the life he has left? Instead, Hawking has chosen to be grateful for what he can still do, and he continues to make huge contributions to science.

I learned about the possibility of perspective at a very early age and it shaped the way I look at everything. I am adopted, which is one of those life events that can produce a jumble of emotions, both good and bad. I was a little girl, between three and four years old, when my parents sat me down on our deck one summer evening and told me. Mom recalls that the conversation took place just before dinner. Dad was still in his suit from work, and we all sat down for crackers and cheese and drinks (mine was always a glass of tonic, which I thought was very grown-up!) as we always did. I was sitting on my mom's lap, enjoying my pre-dinner snack, when she spoke up.

"Kaitlin, you are adopted," she said. (That's my mom, straight to the point, no frills. I love that about her.) "Do you know what that means?"

"No," I said, sipping my drink.

My parents went on to explain it to me. A very nice lady had actually given birth to me, they said. But when I was still a tiny baby I had come to live with them because they had more love in their hearts than they knew what to do with and they wanted to share it with me. They asked if I had any questions and I shook my head "no." That was pretty much that. Mom said I seemed unfazed by the whole thing. What could have been an earth-shaking moment played out like an ordinary family conversation. I've since read that that's a pretty normal reaction for a child that age.

As I got a little older and began to understand better about how my life began, I instinctively felt grateful to my parents for bringing me into their lives and loving me the way every child deserves to be loved, and also to my birth mother for giving me the opportunity to have the parents I do. I truly believe that God meant for us to be together, and that with them was where I was supposed to be. I'm not sure why I've always looked at my adoption as a gift.

At first, I was probably too young to process that there was an alternative to my way of thinking, so I followed the lead of my parents, and they were always open and positive about it. Later I just accepted it as a footnote in the larger narrative of my life.

I know it's not uncommon for adoptees to grieve the loss of their birth parents, and to feel abandoned, rejected, and as though they are not good enough, because if the person who gave birth to you didn't love you enough to keep you, then who would? I understand how someone can go down that road. But for me, gratitude was the great healer. I'd always just assumed that my birth mother's reasons for giving me up were based in her own selflessness, and her love for me, and her wish for me to have the kind of life she felt she couldn't provide, but I never really knew why she did, and I didn't dwell on it. Whenever I did think about my birth mother, I chose to think of her as a blessing.

For most of my life, I didn't know anything about her or the circumstances that led to my being put up for adoption. All I knew was that I was born on Halloween in 1983 and spent the next few weeks with a caretaker until my birth mother's legal right to change her mind expired, and I was finally free to be adopted. It was only much later that I learned she'd written letters to the adoption agency and the courts waiving her right to the waiting period so that I could move on to my permanent home, but the law is the law.

My adoptive parents finally got to take me home in the early afternoon of December 23 when I was almost two months old. (I reference them as "adoptive" for the purpose of clarity. They are my parents.) They named the day Kate's Day, which we still celebrate today. They were my saviors and I was theirs. That's really where my story begins, when I went home with my parents. Ironically, my dad's mother, who lived with my parents toward the end of her life, had passed away in her sleep only hours before my homecoming. When they arrived home with me at around 1:00 that afternoon and waited for their family members to arrive to meet the new baby girl, my parents held me and wept. "Are these tears of happiness or sorrow?" my father asked. My parents agreed that they were both. One life ends, another begins. What a bittersweet moment it was for my mom and dad, suffering the loss of a beloved parent at the same time they were receiving the child they had wanted for so long. Yet even in their grief, my parents found room for joy.

My dad said on that first night I slept in a bassinet at the foot of their bed and they got almost no sleep, listening to my breathing. On my second day home, they decided to give me my first bath. Instructions on how to bathe your new-born were strewn over the kitchen counter. Dad placed a small tub in the kitchen sink and Mom began to read him the directions. Lay out a towel and a clean diaper . . . Make sure the room is warm so your baby doesn't catch a chill . . . Fill the tub with two to three inches of water and test the water temperature on the inside of your wrist . . . Slip your baby into the water feetfirst. Check. Check. Check. Check. While Mom observed, Dad bathed me. When they were finished, they wrapped me in a cozy blanket, "proud as pea-cocks," Dad says, that they'd succeeded at their first task as parents. The moment passed when they suddenly realized they'd forgotten to use soap. They were off to a rocky start, but at least they were able to laugh about it.

What wonderful, loving people my parents are, although as different as night and day. Mom is stoic. She doesn't wear her emotions on her sleeve, but she's the kindest woman I know and she'd do anything for anyone. She rarely expresses her feelings with words, but she's always made me feel more loved than anyone else on earth. Everything my mom does, she does quietly, whether it's work for her church, or volun-teering at a soup kitchen, or coming to school with me dur-ing our first week back after the tragedy. Her actions speak for her giving nature. Dad, on the other hand, has emotions oozing from his pores. He's all warmth and affection, which he expresses with words and great big bear hugs. You don't have to ask how he's feeling, because he always tells you. He's as open and outgoing as Mom is guarded and reserved. Even politically they fall at opposite ends of the spectrum. Dad's a conservative Republican. Mom's a liberal Democrat. (That made for some interesting dinner conversations. "You're voting for who?")

I know that nobody's life is picture perfect, but my childhood was pretty close. I grew up on a dead-end street in a middle-class neighborhood in Connecticut with lots of kids my age to play with. During the warmer months I was always outside, riding my bike, or climbing around in my tree house, or playing games such as SPUD (which is kind of like ball tag) or capture the flag (where the goal is to capture the opposing team's hidden flag). I'd stay out for hours, until Dad showed up on the front porch with his plastic whistle to call me in for dinner. I loved being an only child and having my parents all to myself. They both doted on me.

Saturday mornings were father-daughter time. While Mom gardened or did household chores, Dad and I ran errands, dropping off the recycling, gassing up the car (only at Mobil, that was Dad's rule), picking up groceries (and always two Almond Joys—one for him, one for me). On the way back home we'd pass a McDonald's and Dad always stopped and ordered a large fries and two apple pies, my favorites, all for me. Mom wasn't a shopper, so sometimes Dad would take me to the mall and give me an allowance to spend. (I prided myself on making the most of the money and, even as a little kid, I always picked through the sale and clearance racks, looking for a steal.) Dad was always so much fun to be around.

Mom was a nurturer. Whenever I was hurt or upset, she held me on her lap to comfort me. When I woke up frightened in the middle of the night, she crawled into bed with me (once, for two months straight!). When I needed a good talking-to, Mom would do it, and when I needed help with homework, that was Mom, too. Every night after dinner, we sat together at the dining room table as she patiently went over my school assignments with me. Mom studied English in college, and she was a stickler for grammar and spelling. Still is. She showed me the right way to do things, but I had to do my own work. I remember trying to learn the states and capitals. I just couldn't get it right. Mom finally bought flashcards, and every night we'd go over and over them. I could fidget and complain all I wanted, but Mom wouldn't budge. "We need to get this done," she'd say, calmly, but in a way so I knew I wouldn't win. "It might take some time, but we'll work on it together until you get it." Education was as important in our household as practicing proper manners. Even my place mat was a map, so that while I was eating my breakfast, I might learn something. Looking back, and especially now as I teach, I understand there was a method to Mom's madness and I'm grateful that she taught me the value of learning. But at the time, all I really wanted to do was go outside and ride my bike.

Our extended family included my dad's brother and his wife and my mom's family. My mom is the oldest of five sisters, and they were all very close. I have three cousins on my mother's side and, growing up, we were more like siblings. Every summer, mom and her sisters rented a beach house, usually in Cape Cod or Maine or on the New Jersey shore, and we'd all spend time there. We celebrated birthdays and anniversaries and graduations and holidays together, whenever we could. Holidays were family days. Mom had Thanksgiving at our house. Easter was at one of my aunts' homes and Christmas was always at my grandparents' place. We were a tight-knit group and I never felt as though I was anything other than a whole part of it. Even many years later, when my birth mother sought me out and I finally met her, nothing about that changed. But more about that later. A family is bound, not by blood but by love. That is one of the great lessons my parents taught me, one I likely would not have learned had it not been for the decision by my birth mother to let me go.

But perhaps the most profound lesson I got from my parents, and the one that has carried me through the most difficult chapters of my life, is that your outlook determines how you react to everything. You can curse the rainy day or appreciate the beautiful flowers that result from it, they said.

I can't imagine giving a child a greater gift than that.

8 Snowberry Lane

Growing up, I spent hours sitting at the top of the staircase at my grandparents' house, staring down at a picture that hung in the middle of the wall on the landing below. The picture was a half-moon on a black background. Sometimes when I looked at it I saw the moon. Other times, a woman's face stared back at me. What I eventually came to realize was that what I saw depended on my perspective. On what set of eyes I was looking through on that particular day. Did I want to see the moon, or was I looking for the woman? What I sought was what I saw.

That picture now hangs next to the door in my home. I look at it every time I come and go. Not only is the picture a constant reminder of happy times from childhood, and my wonderful grandparents, but it is also a reminder of the precious family values I might not have learned had my parents not invited me into their family.

My grandparents' house on Snowberry Lane in Wilton, Connecticut, was tucked away on a leafy cul-de-sac, next to a stream that I played in. It was a big brick and cedar shake colonial with white shutters and a screened porch on the side. The porch was my favorite spot. I loved the white wicker furniture with baby-blue cushions that were fashioned after the outside décor at the Breakers resort hotel in Palm Beach, my grandmother's favorite getaway. As a child, I spent countless hours on that porch, sitting in my very own child's version of the wicker chairs, eating my lunch, or coloring, or reading my favorite books (*Curious George* or *Mrs. Piggle-Wiggle* when I was very young; *Matilda* and *Harriet the Spy* as I got a little older; then I turned into an adolescent and I was "too cool" to read). It was such a quiet, peaceful spot that sometimes even a slight summer breeze sounded as loud as a swarm of bees.

My grandmother was a woman of few words. She let her actions speak for her. I always knew that baking for others was her way of showing love. Grandma was always teaching me new recipes. Her favorite sugar cookies (when she turned away, I sprinkled mine with extra Red Hots); the tiny blueberry muffins she called "cupcakes"; her special zucchini bread (it was my job to shave the zucchini and squeeze out the liquid, which I still love doing when I make her recipe in my own kitchen). We usually baked until lunchtime. Then, while my grandfather read or watched a Yankees game on TV (he was a die-hard Yankees fan), my grandmother and I went to town to her garden club, where she had her own vegetable patch, and weeded and picked whatever was ripe to use for dinner that night. By around 4:00, when my grandfather, who was head usher at his church, headed out to Mass, my grandmother and I would be just getting back home and ready for our afternoon nap. We'd curl up on the living room couch and I'd rub her neck to help her fall asleep, but I was the one who usually dozed off first. Before we knew it, Grandpa was walking back in the door, all spiritually refreshed, and it was time for dinner and *Jeopardy!* Once he passed, I made a point to go to his church so I could experience the place that had been so important to him.

Those times with my grandparents were some of the happiest of my life. I wish they could have lasted forever. My grandfather passed away while I was in college. It was my first experience with losing a loved one, and the pain of realizing I would never look into his loving eyes again, or feel the warmth of his smile, was numbing. Three years later, my grandmother followed him. She suffered with Alzheimer's disease, and every week when I visited her she seemed to have less of a grasp on reality. She'd often be confused and have trouble verbalizing her thoughts. Yet she never forgot me, her granddaughter. And she still called me Kaitlin Mary.

Whenever I start to feel the void left by their passing, and it is vast, I close my eyes and imagine those times on Snowberry Lane. When I do, I can see my grandfather, dapper in his suit and hat, walking out the door to usher at his church. I see my grandmother, standing over the kitchen counter, patiently teaching me how to whisk batter, or grease a cookie sheet, or squeeze the juice from a zucchini. Those simple acts had so much meaning for me. They were life lessons.

My grandparents taught me that a well-lived life is one in which we take what is best in us and use it for a higher purpose. That was the way in which they chose to see life. That was their perspective. Be kind to others. Give them your time, which is your love. Whether that means working through God, as my grandfather did with his church, or making homemade baked goods to bring joy to someone else, it's all the same. It's about finding the love from within and sharing it.

In his book *The Purpose Driven Life*, Pastor Rick Warren wrote: "When you give someone your time, you are giving them a portion of your life that you'll never get back. Your time is your life. That is why the greatest gift you can give someone is your time. It is not enough just to *say* relationships are important; we must prove it by investing time in them. Words alone are worthless. *'My children, our love should not be just words and talk; it must be true love, which shows itself in action.'* Relationships take time and effort, and the best way to spell love is 'T-I-M-E.'"

I can count on one hand the times my grandmother said the words "I love you." But my grandparents gave me a part of themselves and that said more than words ever could. It's similar to the end of every school year, when my students move on to the next grade. They're leaving my classroom, but the time we spent together, the feelings we had for each other, the memories we made, will never cease to exist. Those relationships become a part of who we are.

When I look at the picture of the moon on my wall, that's what I see. Not how much I miss my grandparents now that they are no longer physically with me. But the time we spent together, the memories we made, and how grateful I am to them. For sharing their precious time. For showing me the meaning of true love.

For being a part of who I am.

Twenty Miles

My dad always knew my birth mother's name. He'd read it—along with her age and the hospital where I was born—upside down on the paperwork as he and my mother sat across the desk from the woman who was handling my adoption. When he got home that day, he wrote down the information so that if I wanted to learn more about her someday, at least I'd have a starting point.

For as long as I can remember, every so often, Dad offered to help me find my birth mother. The offers always came out of the blue. Each time he asked, I politely declined. "No, Dad. I'm fine," I'd say. After a few years of my father asking me this, I started becoming exasperated and, after a while, usually just shrugged him off. He had good intentions, but I knew everything I wanted to know about my birth mother, or at least what I thought I knew—that she'd had my best interests at heart when she gave me away—and I had no interest in knowing anything more. Then, when I turned twenty-three, my birth mother found me.

Talk about out of the blue. I was living on my own by then and had gone back home one afternoon to have lunch with Mom. We were out on the deck, eating the sandwiches she'd fixed for us, when, without even a transition from whatever small talk we were making, she asked if I planned to tell my then boyfriend that I was adopted. At that point, I hadn't told anyone. Not my boyfriend, not even my very closest girlfriends. My only reason for keeping my adoption to myself was to protect my parents from anyone thinking of them as anything other than what they were: my mom and my dad.

"Well," I said, "I haven't really thought about it much. But if he and I were to get engaged I would tell him, for no other reason than if we planned on having children I'd want him to know that I didn't know my familial history." Mom nodded, and without saying a word, she stood up from the table and went inside. A minute later, she returned, holding a large manila envelope in her hand. "Well, I think you can know that," she said, handing me the envelope. "Here you go." I sensed my mom's discomfort. In retrospect, I understand what she must have been feeling. She is my mother and I am her daughter and she didn't want anything to get in the way of that. At that moment, though, I didn't have a clue about what she was handing me. If anything, I thought that maybe the envelope contained copies of health records she'd gotten from my birth mother's doctor and held on to until I was old enough to have them.

I put my hand in the envelope and pulled out the contents, a stack of letters, all addressed to my mom, all with the same Westport return address. I looked at Mom, pulled out one of the letters, and started reading.

"Many times over the years I've tried to look for you and Kaitlin, but have never been able to find you. I was told early on that you had moved out of state. I never thought I could find you."

Mom sat there quietly as I finished reading and opened a second letter. "I wanted you to know her birth father and I married and live only a few miles from you."

Then, a third letter. "Kaitlin has a sister."

I looked at my mom blankly. "Hmm. That's interesting," I said. My dispassionate reaction might seem odd, especially to people who are not familiar with adoptees, but I really wasn't feeling much. I think that, had I not been so loved by my parents, maybe the letters would have tugged at me more. But I had my happy family. I didn't need another mother or another father.

———

I was intrigued that I had a sibling. I'd always wondered what it would be like to have a sister to share things with, and I'd even fabricated one back in the fifth grade. "Kristy" was a central character in many of the entries I made in the weekly journal we kept for Mrs. Beaulier's class. "Kristy and I went to the mall over the weekend. Kristy and I went to see a movie with our parents. Kristy and I went on vacation to Maine with our cousins. Eventually I was found out when my parents attended a parent-teacher conference and Mrs. Beaulier asked how my sister, Kristy, was doing. You can imagine my parents' surprise. "Kristy? Kaitlin is an only child. She doesn't have a sister." (That story came in handy many years later when I asked about the sister of one of my first-graders and her flabbergasted parents told me there was no sister. "Don't worry," I said. "I did the same thing when I was little." That seemed to appease them.)

In one of the letters, my birth mother floated the idea of meeting me at some point. "So when do you think you should meet her?" Mom asked. I felt like I was walking a tightrope. I feared that if I agreed to meet my birth mother, my mom might feel hurt. That was the last thing I wanted. On the other hand, I didn't want to push my birth mother away if she needed to see me. Who was I to deny her? And I confess, I was curious about my sister. *Does she look like me?* I wondered. *Does she have a similar personality? Does she know about me?* "Well," I said, "if she wants to meet me, I'll meet her."

My mom set up the meeting by e-mail. The arrangement she'd made was that I was to meet my birth mother at the restaurant where my family celebrated Kate's Day every year, as well as birthdays and anniversaries and other special occasions. It was halfway between where I lived and my birth mother's home in Westport.

Two weeks later, I was walking through the door of the restaurant, looking for someone who looked like me. The restaurant was crowded, and I probably wouldn't have known my birth mother if she hadn't stood up to greet me. I don't look anything like her. I felt strangely ambivalent as we hugged.

"It's nice to meet you," I said.

She nodded and smiled. "I can't believe how tall you are! Your sister is short and tiny and I'd just assumed you'd look the same way."

We sat down across the table from each other. She started the conversation by asking questions about my life, questions she'd been storing up for twenty-three years. She asked about my childhood and what it was like growing up. What kinds of things did I do? Had I played sports? Had lots of friends? What were my high school years like? My college experience? What was my favorite food? She seemed nice and she was easy to talk to.

When I'd answered everything she asked, she volunteered the details of my adoption. She said she was in high school when she became pregnant with me. Times were different then. Having a child out of wedlock could bring unwanted attention to a family, and she had younger siblings as well. Her mother and her discussed and agreed that it would be better for her to go away until it was time for her to deliver me. It was all very quiet, and shortly after my birth she had returned to high school to finish up. She'd eventually married my birth father, and they had my sister nine years after she'd given birth to me.

"All these years, I wondered about you," she said. "I wondered if you were okay, if you were happy, if you had the life I envisioned for you."

My birth mother said she had tried to find me over the years, but she had nothing to go on and my adoption records were legally sealed. When she'd asked the adoption agency for help in finding me, they told her we'd moved out of state, they couldn't say where. Of course, we hadn't gone anywhere. I lived in the same house my whole life, as it turned out, just twenty miles from her. When her search for me hit a dead end, she'd stopped looking for me. Then, as my sister got older, and she prepared to tell her about me, my birth mother resumed her search, this time with the help of the Internet and better luck. A few months before she'd started writing letters to my mom, someone she'd met online had provided her with information that finally led to me. My birth mother said she was thankful that my mother showed me her letters and that I'd agreed to meet with her. "I wanted to meet you to see if I'd made the right decision," she said.

I thanked her for reaching out to my mom and for being curious about how my life had turned out, and I assured her that my childhood couldn't have been better. Relatively speaking, it was idyllic. "Honestly," I said, "if you had never looked for me, we would never have met, because I wouldn't have looked for you." I wasn't trying to be callous or insensitive, and my birth mother didn't take it that way. She interpreted my statement exactly as I'd meant it: You can rest assured that you made the right decision. Thank you for that. I have had a blessed life. "That's the best gift you could ever have given me," she said. I smiled. "And thank you for the gift you gave me," I said.

We left the restaurant that night promising to stay in touch, and we have. I've met my birth father, but they have since divorced, and my sister and I have developed a friendship. I've met most of my blood relatives and my birth family has spent time with our family. I like having all these new people in my life. It's as if I've inherited a whole new group of friends.

I think I miscalculated the impact that meeting my birth mother would have on my life. What it did, and I'm not sure why, was give me the freedom to tell people I'm adopted. Of course, when I told my friends, most of them already knew because my dad had mentioned it to their parents somewhere along the way. My parents had never kept my adoption a secret.

But even more than feeling confident about talking about my adoption, meeting my birth mother confirmed what I had chosen to believe all along: that the reason for my adoption had nothing to do with rejection or a lack of caring on her part. My birth mother let me go out of selflessness and love. And in doing so, she opened the door for me to have the beautiful life I have.

Just recently, I asked my birth mom to reflect for a moment on that first meeting. This is what she wrote:

> *One of the best moments of my life was when you walked in. I still remember like it was last night.*
>
> *Loved seeing you, I think part of me expected you to be a little girl as the only picture I'd ever had of you was when you were one and here you were, walking in . . .*
> *TALL and beautiful, not the sweet little girl from the*

*picture I'd looked at every day for the past 20+ years but
a young woman and you were blonde, like my sisters.*

*Everyone always asks me about our first meeting and
they always assume that I cried . . . no tears for me, just
pure happiness . . . I couldn't stop smiling.*

*Loved that we just sat and talked and talked . . .
meant the world to me.*

*What stands out the most from that evening was how
completely content you were/are. Made me so happy.*

*And one of the best things that you'd said to me was
that if I hadn't found you, you didn't know if you'd ever
have looked for me . . . this made me happy for so many
reasons! I knew from that comment that you had/have
wonderful parents who loved you so much that there was
never any doubt for you, that you didn't feel resentment
towards me. For the previous 24 years before we'd met, I
would think of you every day and offer a prayer that you
were happy, loved, well cared for and didn't hate me.*

*And in that moment, I knew you had been/were. I
knew that I'd made the right choice for myself and, most
importantly, for YOU! I knew.*

I often think about how different my life might have been
had my birth mother decided to keep me. I can't even fathom
it. I would never have known my parents. I would be an

entirely different person. And I think about how, all those years before she told me the circumstances of my adoption, I could have chosen to believe the worst, and where would that have gotten me, except perhaps bitter and angry? Instead, having been guided by my parents, I made the choice to take what life gave me and find the abundant good in it, and to be grateful for the blessings.

Just recently, my dad found a card my birth mother had written and sent along with me. "Please don't be scared," she wrote. "All my love and happiness to you always." With those words, my birth mother sent me home to my family. I wouldn't be who I am today without them and the life they gave me.

And I know that I am exactly where God intended for me to be all along.

MY DARKEST

HOUR

"What lies behind us and what lies before us are tiny matters compared to what lies within us."

—Henry S. Haskins

December 14, 2012

The morning sun rising over Long Island Sound on December 14 was even more breathtaking than usual. That big, red ball, pitched against a cloudless blue sky, was so striking that I stopped on my way out of the house, dropped my lunch bag and car keys on the kitchen counter, and grabbed my phone to snap a few pictures. My step had a skip as I pushed out the door and walked to my car to head to school. Could life get any better? I was twenty-nine years old, engaged to the man of my dreams, and working in a job I would have done for free, I loved it so much.

As I pulled out of the driveway to begin the drive to Newtown, my thoughts returned to the previous weekend when my mom and I traveled from Greenwich to Westhampton to make wedding preparations. It had been a magical weekend.

First, we'd met with a florist and chosen all white roses and dahlias and hydrangeas for the flower arrangements, then we'd gone to the beach and booked the date for the following August at a beautiful place called the Ocean-bleu. The restaurant is built high on the dunes and, standing there, looking out over the water, I had pictured my dad and I taking that long walk down the beach to where Nick and our guests would be waiting. The following day, we'd met Dad and Nick for our annual Christmas brunch and gone over all our plans. I could hardly wait for summer to come, but first we had the holidays to look forward to.

The drive to Sandy Hook took fifty minutes on a good day on I-84, and that day traffic was light. Taking exit 10 off I-84, as usual, I meandered through the Newtown country-side, excited to start the day. As I turned onto Dickinson Drive, I glanced at my dashboard clock. It was 7:45. I parked my car in the teachers' lot, reached for my pile of books and papers, and proceeded to the school's main entrance, through the double doors, past the main office, and across the hall to my classroom. Dropping my books on my desk, I went right to work. Our reading specialist was coming to observe my class and I wanted to make sure everything was ready for her visit. The year before, Sandy Hook had adopted the Reading Workshop program, which gives students the tools they need for more independent reading and comprehension skills. The reading specialist was scheduled to arrive at 9:45 and spend an hour or so monitoring how the program was working, specifically, whether the students were engaged in what they were reading and thinking critically about what they had read. It was an important day for my students and me, and I wanted to make sure everything was in order. For instance, that their reading bins had the proper material, and that the lesson I'd prepared for the workshop was comprehensive enough. I was so busy that I hadn't even taken the time to greet a group of my coworkers as they walked back and forth between the main office and a nearby conference room where a meeting was being held. By the time the buses arrived and my students filed into our classroom, a few minutes before nine, I felt ready for the day. At 9:10, like clockwork, the announcements came over the PA system, followed by the Pledge of Allegiance and a moment of silence.

"Good morning, Fantastic Friends!" I said, just before taking attendance.

"Good morning, Miss Roig!" they replied.

Only one of my students was missing—a boy who was away skiing with his family. After attendance, my students settled in to do their morning work until I played the song to signal morning meeting. They gathered around my chair, excited to get started. I picked up a pile of cards, each one with a different greeting written on it, and fanned them out the way a magician does a deck of playing cards before a magic trick. The cards said things like *¡Hola!* and *Bonjour* and *High Five!* One student picked a card from the deck, and whatever was written on it was the day's greeting. The student with the card then greeted the classmate seated beside him or her, and then that child greeted the next child in the circle, and so on. I always reminded my students that when they were greeting one another to look their classmates in the eyes, speak kindly, and offer a firm but not too hard handshake.

That morning, the card chosen was *Ball Roll*, a special card and one of the kids' favorites, which meant they got to roll a ball to one another as they said their good mornings. The student seated next to me was always excited about being able to greet the teacher. That morning, it was the little girl with cascades of brown curly hair who always wore pink. "Good morning, Miss Roig," she said, in her tinkling first-grade voice. I loved that moment. You can't help but be happy after looking into the eager eyes of a sweet, smiling first-grader.

After that, we moved on to sharing time, a few minutes when the students got to share personal stories with one another. Because the Christmas season and Hanukkah were upon us, the theme that day was "Our Holiday Traditions." One of my students, a rambunctious boy with chestnut-colored eyes and foot-long lashes, smart as a whip, had been chattering about Christmas since September, and now it was just eleven days away. He was wild with anticipation. He told the story of his cousins coming to spend the holidays, squealing as he spoke. (For the last three months, when it was his turn, he told the same story, but his classmates didn't seem to mind, or, if they did, they were kind enough not to say so!) As was our routine, three students got to share stories and the others were expected to make comments and ask questions. The others talked about making cookies, and visiting Santa, and listening for reindeer, and lighting the menorah, and visits with family members and friends. At the end of each presentation the storyteller addressed his or her classmates, saying, "Thank you for my comments and questions." It was an important way of instilling in the children the appropriate way to share and speak with their peers.

Next on the schedule was Morning Message, a time when we discussed what the day was to bring. That day, of course, we talked about the visit from our reading specialist and how important it was for us to impress her with our reading skills. "Let's get excited about today!" I said. "You're going to shine!" It was 9:30, fifteen minutes before the "big test." The students were eager to show off their reading skills and the books they had tucked in their bags, ready to read.

But we never got that far.

FIRST COMES the initial blast of gunfire, then the sound of shattering glass. The hair on my arms stands up. I know right away what I am hearing. Columbine is happening in the place we called Pleasantville. How can it be? Someone with a weapon is shooting their way into our perfect school. My classroom is the first one in the building. *We are in grave danger,* I think, *sitting targets.* I jump up, run to the door, pull it closed, and switch off the lights. Thank God for the piece of dark blue construction paper I taped to the door window months ago in preparation for a lockdown drill and forgot to take down. I can't lock the door. My keys are clear across the room, on top of my desk, and there's no time to fetch them. For what? A locked door is no match for a magazine of bullets. If we're going to live, we have to find a hiding place. Fast. I look around the classroom. My students don't seem to understand what is happening. One, the little girl I call our fashionista, because she wears things like leopard prints and leggings, stands there smiling. I can't tell if she is somehow oblivious to the sounds or scared frozen. The windows don't open wide enough for a first-grader to climb through, and who knows what or who is waiting outside? Evil is coming for us and there's nowhere to go.

Where can we hide? Where can we hide? There's only one place. The bathroom—a tiny, tiny first grade–sized lavatory with only a toilet and a toilet-paper dispenser inside. Its dimensions are about the size of two first-grade desks pushed together. Maybe three feet by four feet. There is so little space that the sink is on the outside, in the classroom. I have never even been inside of the bathroom before. An adult wouldn't fit comfortably. How in God's name will I get sixteen of us in there? It is our only chance. The impossible will have to become possible.

Everything is happening so quickly. We are under siege. I turn to my students, who look up at me with pleading eyes. "Into the bathroom! Now!" I say.

At first they protest. "In there?" "How?" "Why?" "What do you mean, Miss Roig?"

"Bathroom! Now!" I say, repeating myself. They understand that the teacher means business. I rush them toward the back of the classroom. Shots are being fired outside our classroom door. There's no time. "Hurry!" I say, pushing them into the tiny space with the toilet in the center. "Hurry!" But I know that no matter how quickly my students respond, it will still take two or three minutes to get everyone inside, minutes I feel sure we don't have.

We all push into the bathroom, and when there isn't a millimeter of space left, I begin lifting my students and piling them inside. I place one student, then two, then three on top of the toilet and hoist up my littlest girl and sit her on the toilet-paper dispenser. We are all crushed together with not even enough room left to take a deep breath. I reach out to pull the door closed, but the door isn't there. Oh my God. In my rush to try to save us, I didn't even notice. The door opens into the bathroom. We are blocking it with our bodies. I feel myself beginning to panic. Here we are, stuffed into a room, with a madman bearing down on us, and the door that is supposed to hide us is obstructed by us and can't close.

My heart pounds against my chest, but I cannot afford to lose my composure, not if we are to have any chance of getting out of this alive. First-graders model their teacher's behavior. If I panic, they'll all panic, and we'll be dead. One by one, I pick up the students who are blocking the door and move each one behind it until I am finally able to push it closed. But just before I do, I reach outside for a large storage cabinet on wheels that is nearby and pull it as close as I can to the front of the bathroom door, hoping that maybe it will conceal the door. "Now," I say, "we have to be absolutely quiet. We can't say a word." I can't help but wonder if, by trapping us in the bathroom, I have just sentenced us to certain death. What if the shooter realizes that the storage cabinet is a ruse and shoots right through it?

Someone shouts, "Shooter! Stay put!" Is that our principal? The school nurse? Another teacher? The sounds are too muffled to tell. Then, ear-splitting, rapid-fire shots, like a machine gun—*di-di-di-di-di-di-di-di-di-di-di-di*—over and over and over. We hear pleading. My students stay perfectly quiet. First-graders are black-and-white. They understand that someone very bad is searching for us and in order for us not to be discovered they stay perfectly quiet. In our silence, we hear voices, although whose is unclear. They are muffled voices. People are pleading for their lives. "No! Please, no! Please! No!" If my students are to keep even relatively calm, they must not know that my insides are shaking and I'm sure we are all about to die. It's a very difficult thing, putting on a cool front in the midst of what I know is life and death. With the inescapable sounds of carnage happening all around us, my little ones are feeling desperate. "What is happening?" one of them whispers. My fashionista begins to cry. I cup her face in my hands and look into her teary eyes. "We're going to be okay," I promise. I never make promises I can't keep, especially not to children, but this is a matter of life and death. The boy who straddles the top of the toilet is shaking so hard that he accidently flushes. Once, then again. We all hold our breath. *Shhhhhhhhhh!!!!! Did the shooter hear?* I look at the boy and his face says it all. *I'm scared and I'm sorry and I don't know what to do.* "Miss Roig, I don't want to die today," one of my students whispers. "I just want my mom," another one says, fighting tears. "I don't want to die before Christmas," says my student who has been talking about the holiday for months. We are squeezed together like fingers in a tight fist. My kids want out of this sweltering, sealed-up box we're in. "I'll lead the way!" one of the boys whispers. "I know karate," says another boy. Hadn't it been only moments ago that he told us the story of finding a dollar under his pillow for his two front teeth? "No," I say gently. "There are bad guys out there and we need to wait for the good guys to come." I can't bear to think that their last moments will be spent this way: in fear. I must reassure them, even though I don't believe my own words. "It's going to be okay. We're going to be okay," I say. Then, because I believe that death is imminent and I want to do whatever I can to make them feel safe, I tell them how much they have meant to me. "I need you to know that I love you all very much," I say. In comforting them, I have also brought comfort to myself. "Anyone who believes in the power of prayer needs to pray right now," I say, "and anyone who does not needs to think really happy thoughts." I put my hands together and start to pray. The kids are too crammed together to move their arms, but most of them close their eyes and I assume they are following my instruction. The shooting continues. Now I am prepared to die.

IT's BEEN QUIET for a while now. Eerily quiet. How can a school that I know had been full of people this morning be absolutely silent now? *Where is everyone?* It seems like just my students and me are left in the building. I feel isolated and profoundly alone. I wonder if the gunman is lurking outside our door, waiting for us to feel safe enough to come out of the bathroom and fall into his trap. So much time has passed that it feels like forever. I worry that we may run out of air. *If the good guys were coming, they would have been here by now, wouldn't they? Why is it so deathly quiet?* I think about my beloved fiancé and all the plans we've made for our future together. He suffered so much when he lost his mother, I'm not sure he can survive the tragedy of losing me. Nick needs me, and so do my loving, devoted parents. I worry that they will not be able to handle my death. I think about my students' parents and the unimaginable grief they will suffer because I was powerless to save their children. My worst fear is that I will see my class murdered before I die and I won't be able to stop it. All we can do now is wait.

An eternity passes. The bathroom is stifling and my armpits are soaked with sweat. Some of my kids are becoming impatient. "I'm hot, Miss Roig," one whispers. "Can we please get out?" asks another. Several say they need to go to the bathroom. For the most part, though, they are quite content to be quiet if it means the bad guy can't find us. I wonder what is happening outside. Does the silence mean the shooter is gone? Or is he preparing for his next move? Then, from the other side of the wall, come the voices of people who are barking orders. I hear them clearly. "Don't look up." "Don't open your eyes." "Walk quickly." *Oh my God. Is there more than one shooter? Are they kidnapping people? What is going to happen to us? My heart races in my chest. My kids look up at me.* "Shhhhhhhh," I say. We have been in the bathroom for a very long time. At least forty-five minutes. The heat is becoming unbearable. We can barely take a deep breath.

A knock comes at the door and we all stiffen with fear. I put my index finger to my lips. I fear that if we make any noise, the shooter will realize that the teacher has hidden her whole class in here. "Ask who's there," I whisper to one of my students. I don't want the shooter to know that there are sixteen terrified people huddled together behind the bathroom door. "Who is it?" my little guy asks. I can hear the quiver in his voice. "Hey, little fella," someone replies. The man sounds kind, but I am unconvinced. "We're here to help you," he says. "Unlock the door." *No way*, I think. Why in the world would I trust the words of a faceless stranger? No way am I going to risk opening the door for a killer. Now, I speak. "If you really are the police, I need your badge," I say. Seconds pass. A badge is slipped under the door. I pick it up and examine it. It looks fake, like a play badge that one of my students might wear. I desperately want for it to be real, but I'm not convinced. "This doesn't look real," I say. "I don't believe you." I look around at my kids and I know they are thinking what I am. *Please let this be the good guys.* One little girl is choking back tears. I take her face in my hands and smile. If she starts to cry, the others will cry. I can't let that happen, not until I find out who is on the other side of the door. "If you are the police and you're here to help us, then you should have the key to this door. Or you should be able to get it," I say. A few more minutes pass before I hear the rattle of keys. I hear the scraping sound of a key going into the lock. It doesn't work. Another key, another failed attempt. Then five and six and seven tries. My stomach churns with each twist of the lock. My students' eyes are wide.

The tenth key works. The knob turns and the door pushes

in. I see an army of uniforms—people dressed in black and wearing helmets and carrying big guns, peering in at us. A SWAT team is in our classroom. The good guys are here. I am flooded with feelings of relief and gratitude. They look as surprised to see all of us as we are to see them. I think they were expecting to see one child, not the teacher and her entire class. I've never been so happy to see anyone in my life.

They pull us out of the bathroom, at first, one by one, until there is enough room for us to move on our own. Our heroes lead us out of the classroom and guide us in the opposite direction of the bodies in the hallway and the bloodstained floor. I grab the hands of the two students closest to me and follow the instructions to "go. Fast." We rush the students down the hall and out of the building. "Where is the bad guy?" I ask as we make our way to the firehouse. *Is he still lurking here, somewhere, ready to hurt us?* They assure me that we are safe. I say "Thank you" over and over. "Thank you for finding us in that tiny bathroom." "Thank you for being the good guys." "Thank you for saving our lives."

The Firehouse

Our rescuers lead us across the parking lot and around the corner to the old brick firehouse, where we go during evacuation drills. But the scene there is anything but controlled and organized the way it is during practices and drills. Inside, it is chaos. We are the last class in. At first we are taken to a holding area. I worry, even though I have been reassured that we are safe, that someone is going to burst in shooting. Finally, we are escorted to a larger room where the rescued students are lined up by grade and by class to wait to be claimed. We are ushered to the first-grade section.

Looking around, I see a bizarre dichotomy of emotions. Some people are running around in a frenzy, searching the faces in the crowd for loved ones. Some are crying. Others are chatting amiably. I hear the sound of cartoons playing (perhaps to soothe our traumatized children?). Someone is on his phone, ordering pizzas and sodas. *Who thinks of ordering pizza at a time like this?* I am incredulous, unaware that most of the people here have no idea what happened inside of that school.

With my students settled, I reach for my cell phone to call Nick and my mom and realize it's back in the classroom, so I borrow a phone from a colleague and dial their numbers, but neither one picks up. A moment later, I borrow someone else's phone and try again. This time, my mom answers. She tells me she has just heard about a shooting at the school and was headed out to meet me. My students are all around me, so I don't want to say too much. "Please, just come as soon as you can," I say.

The parents of my students arrive in quick succession. Mothers and fathers shriek with relief and joy when they spot their children. I am dazed but somehow functioning, going through the motions. Before anyone can leave, I hand the parents a pen and ask that they sign their children out—the way I used to do at the end of a day at summer camp. *This is surreal,* I say to myself. Some of the parents wish me a good weekend before whisking their children away. Some say cheerily, "See you on Monday!" as if nothing has changed.

But everything has changed.

I turn to a fellow first-grade teacher and ask, "How are you?" She looks at me matter-of-factly and replies, "Oh, I'm fine." My eyes fill with tears. "People are dead," I say. "What do you mean?" she asks, disbelieving. "No one died." I would later learn that in those early stages, very few people understood the gravity of the situation. Most had heard either on the television or on the radio or from one another that the worst casualty was a teacher who'd been shot in the foot. Most people were relieved that the damage hadn't been worse. They just didn't know.

I watch the faces of the people who are still waiting and I know that some of them will go home alone. As minutes and then hours pass and they still have no word of their child, or their mother, or their wife, they begin to understand. This is much worse than anyone thought. Yes, this is much, much worse. My students and I know. We heard the voices of our teachers and classmates in the final moments of their lives. When we left our classroom with the SWAT team, the last class out of the building, we saw the dozens of bullet casings on the floor. Spent shells that had rolled under our door from the adjoining classroom, where so many were killed. We heard what went on in there, and outside in the hallway, and in the classroom a little farther down the hall. I wish I could forget those sounds. I pray that one day my kids do.

Little by little, the crowd has dispersed. All my students are gone now, and most of the others are, too. My mom finally arrives. She says it took her nearly an hour to get through the gridlock of cars and emergency vehicles on the streets leading to the school. Some people abandoned their cars when they couldn't get any closer and ran to the firehouse to look for their children. My mom embraces me. She is stoic, as always. Holding on to her, I feel like a child, a frightened child who just wants to get out of this place. Even her reassuring presence doesn't quell the fear that prickles through my body. Once we are cleared to leave, I grab her arm and start running, not knowing that, in a separate room in the firehouse, the families of those who are still unaccounted for are learning their loved ones are gone.

Soon enough, everyone learns what my students and I already know: that many people have lost their lives. I hear the horrific details of what happened outside our classroom from others, people who love me and tell me gently the awful truths of that morning. I am horrified to hear that our principal and the school psychologist were shot to death outside my classroom, where they attempted to tackle the shooter on his way into the school. How very brave they were. The shooter then continued down the hallway to the first-grade classroom two doors away from mine. There, he found a guest teacher and a behavior therapist huddled protectively around their students. He sprayed them with bullets, killing everyone but one little girl who had the wherewithal to play dead. Then he headed back up the hallway toward our classroom, stopping next door, where the first-grade teacher and her aide had just finished hiding their students in closets and cabinets and under the teacher's desk. From what I was told, he appeared at the door just as the teacher was closing it, demanding to know where her students were. I wasn't surprised to hear that she'd tried to convince him that her kids were in the gymnasium on the other side of the school. She would have done anything to protect her students. Still, mercilessly, he killed her and then he fatally shot the students and the special-education aide who were hiding under the desk. The aide was found cradling an autistic child in her arms. When he stopped to reload, the rest of the students in the classroom made a run for it and survived. Innocent first-graders knowing their teachers couldn't help them now, and having to run for their lives. I can't stand to think about what must have been going on in their minds. A moment later, when police began to arrive, the rampage stopped when the killer shot himself in the head and lay dead on the classroom floor. He still had 253 rounds of live ammunition on his body.

That was the classroom that adjoined ours.

The Interview

Drive as fast as you can!" I cried, as my mom slipped behind the wheel of her car. I slid into the passenger seat beside her, furtively scrutinizing our surroundings for any sign of danger. "What if the police lied and the shooter is still out here?" I wondered. "What if there is another shooter that they don't even know about?"

In my mother's haste to get to me, she'd parked in a stranger's driveway and run through the crowds and the traffic tie-ups the rest of the way to the firehouse. Now it seemed like she was backing out in slow-motion.

"Hurry!" I cried. "Mom, please hurry!" I wanted to get out of that driveway. Out of the neighborhood. Out of Newtown altogether. I felt helpless to help myself. The only control I had left was ordering my mom to get out of there. "Hurry, Mom! Please hurry!" I cried, trying to swallow a breath. "Okay, Kaitlin," she said in her perpetually steady way.

For my whole life, my mom was able to calm me down with her cool manner and soothing voice. Not now. She didn't yet know what my class and I went through, that we were living in a different world from the one we knew before that morning. My new world was scary. Danger was lurking everywhere. There was no safe haven—not even sitting next to my mom, the woman who was my savior, my protector, my comfort, my strength. If our elementary school wasn't safe, no place was.

"Am I alive?" I asked, my eyes bulging, my heart pounding wildly. "Did we really get out of the bathroom, Mom?" "Am I really here with you?" My mom reassured me. "Yes, Kaitlin, you're alive. You're safe." The fear that shot through my body turned to numbness. For the rest of the ride, I was silent. My emotions were shutting down to protect my sanity. Still, the terrible stirring under my skin let me know that panic loomed just below the surface, ready to emerge at any moment.

We pulled up to my parents' house at about 2:00 p.m. Nick was waiting outside for us. I ran to him and grabbed him so hard that I felt him flinch. "Okay, babe," he said, in a tone that told me he was completely unaware of the enormity of the tragedy or how close my students and I came to losing our lives. Nick led me inside and I dropped onto the living room couch. I couldn't even speak. I just sat there, staring straight ahead. It was as if every ounce of strength had drained from my body and I didn't even have enough juice to move. Neither Nick nor my parents pressed me for details, and I didn't offer any. I just sat there, listening to the telephone ring and ring and ring. Mom answered some of the calls, and some she let go to the answering machine. I didn't have the breath to ask who was calling and she didn't offer.

A little bit of time passed, I don't know how long it was. Mom walked toward me holding the telephone receiver with her hand over the speaker. "It's Diane Sawyer's producer and I think you should talk to her," my mother said. "I think you should hear what she has to say." *What?* I thought to myself. *You want me to talk to the news media?* It was the last thing I expected to hear from my intensely private and discreet mother. I'm sure that's why, after a moment's hesitation, I took the phone from her. I wasn't thinking. I wasn't feeling. I was simply following directions from the person I trusted most in the world. "Hello, this is Kaitlin," I said.

For the next ten minutes the producer talked and I listened. It was the same conversation she'd had earlier with my mom and the reason I suddenly understood why my mother suggested I take the call. The producer started off by telling me that her parents and Sawyer's mother were all teachers. Both she and the anchor had a keen understanding of the sacrifices that good teachers make for their students, she said, and that was never more evident than what had taken place in the classrooms and hallways of Sandy Hook that morning. The news reports were all focused on the shooter, but they wanted to do a piece that showcased the importance of teachers and what they did for their students every day. They had no interest in exploiting the tragedy, nor did they want to focus the broadcast on the monster that caused it. Their interest was in highlighting the love of a teacher for her students in the midst of one of the darkest times ever to befall our nation's schools.

I wavered. "I don't know," I told the producer. "I'm not sure. I can't really think right now." I could see from my mom's expression that she wanted me to do the interview. As uncertain as I was about being on television, I trusted her enough to know there was a reason she was steering me in that direction, and she always only had my best interest at heart. The producer gently prodded me, reiterating the point that the intention of the piece was as a tribute to teachers. Hesitantly, I finally agreed. "Okay," I said.

Sawyer arrived around thirty minutes later. For the next hour, I told her bits and pieces of what I remembered about what my students and I went through that morning. I told her about hearing the shots and breaking glass and rushing my kids into that tiny bathroom. I talked about how good my students were, and that they knew they had to be quiet so the bad guy didn't find us.

"Did you tell them to be quiet?" she asked.

"Oh, yes," I said, my eyes tearing and my voice shaking. "I told them to be absolutely quiet. Because I was just so afraid if he did come in, he would hear us and start shooting the door. I said, 'We have to be absolutely quiet.' And I said, 'There are bad guys out there now.' I just wanted us to be okay. And I was so, so saddened that there are people who in this situation are not okay. And my heart, my heart goes out to anyone who knew them and was part of their lives. I've never been a part of something obviously anywhere near this traumatic. And so I'm hearing the gunfire in the hallway and I'm thinking in my mind, *I'm the first classroom, why isn't he coming?* In my mind, I'm thinking, *As a six- or seven-year-old, what are your thoughts?* I'm thinking that I almost have to be the parent, like I have to tell them—I said to them, 'I need you to know that I love you all very much and that it's going to be okay,' because I thought that was the last thing we were ever going to hear." My words caught in my throat.

"I think there are a lot of people who wish, who want all the teachers to know how much it means to them, how much they care about their children," Sawyer said, wrapping up. I was grateful to have been given the opportunity to honor my colleagues and the students who acted with such bravery and compassion, but I was relieved the interview was over.

As Sawyer stood to leave, I glanced at Nick and my parents, and the stricken expressions on their faces reminded me that my talk with Diane was the first time they'd heard from me what had happened that morning. Before that, they had no idea about the trauma my students and I lived through. Or that we'd been so close to losing our lives.

If it hadn't been for my respect for my mom, I never would have spoken to anyone that afternoon. But once the interview was over, I was convinced that I had made the right decision, because sitting down in a formal interview setting I was able to process my thoughts about what happened and articulate my memories in a way I would not have been able to do otherwise. The people closest to me could finally understand what my students and I had gone through. I'm not sure I would have been able to tell them otherwise, and I know they wouldn't have pressed me for details. And if I was the vehicle through which to deliver the message about the relationship between teachers and their students, then I was grateful to have been given the opportunity, and, in doing so, honoring my colleagues and the students who acted with such bravery and compassion.

———

I wouldn't know it for a long time, but that interview was a way of purging some of the horror I was holding inside, and a tiny first step in what would be a long road to healing. That's why my mom suggested I do it. She knew that all along.

The Day After

I woke up late on Saturday and found Nick sitting on the couch in the living room, the remote in his hand, the TV tuned to CNN. Twenty-four hours had passed since the bloodshed, and the names of colleagues and children who'd lost their lives were beginning to trickle out. I couldn't bring myself to watch the first-day coverage, but after I'd collapsed into bed, depleted from talking and crying and trying to stifle my anguish with an extra glass of wine, Nick had stayed up for most of the night, watching the news. He looked dead tired. I was still feeling numb. I'm sure it was my body's way of helping me cope. Had I been able to access the feelings of sorrow and anger and revulsion that festered inside me, I might have lost my mind.

I sat down next to Nick, still in a daze. "Are you sure you

want to see this?" he asked. I didn't answer. All of the major news stations were broadcasting a press conference with Connecticut State Police lieutenant Paul Vance. He was saying something about the medical examiner getting ready to release the official list of names of the people who had been killed, but I was having trouble comprehending his words. To me, he sounded far away, as if he were speaking from the other end of a tunnel. His mouth moved in slow motion and his sentences slurred into a kind of indiscernible drone. I glanced at the news crawler at the bottom of the screen: "Twenty-six dead, including twenty children. All victims have been ID'd." I felt sick to my stomach. Knowing the names of everyone who didn't make it out of our school wasn't something I was ready to hear. The official list would just confirm what my students and I already knew from listening to the horror firsthand outside our classroom. Our community had suffered an enormous loss and we didn't need names to begin mourning.

Why those kind women, who had devoted themselves to helping groom our children to grow up to be thoughtful, caring adults? Why innocent first-graders, little ones, who still believed in the Tooth Fairy, for God's sake? Our school was a tightly knit community unto itself. It was inevitable that my students and I had lost people we knew. People we cared for. We heard it when we were holed up in that tiny bathroom. (Later, when I allowed myself to hear more, I learned that my principal, a sibling of one of my students, and the teacher and half of the first-grade class whose room adjoined ours were all among the lost. That took the tragedy to an even deeper level.)

The reporters were shouting questions at Lieutenant Vance, most of them about the shooter. What was his motive? Did he leave anything behind that might answer why he did this? What about the "secondary crime scene," the shooter's house (where he'd shot and killed his mother before coming for us)? Was there any evidence found there that might shed light on his motive? *Why are they focusing on why this person did what he did?* I wondered. There is no answer for the havoc he wrought on our community. Nothing can explain his viciousness.

"Can we please turn it off?" I asked, turning to Nick.

As numb as I was emotionally, physically my insides felt like they were crawling. My chest felt tight, my skin prickled, and I couldn't catch my breath. It felt like I'd had the wind knocked out of me. I was in a perpetual state of fear. I didn't know how to relieve what I was feeling, but I needed to do something to occupy my scrambled mind. I had to stay in motion to keep from becoming completely unglued.

For the next few hours, I never stopped moving. I scrubbed down all of the kitchen appliances and countertops, and scoured the tiles on the bathroom floor. I rearranged furniture, vacuumed the carpets, and polished tabletops that had already been polished to a sheen. I dusted every picture frame in every room and the molding around every doorway. I washed, dried, and folded sheets that had already been washed, dried, and put away. Nick tried to help, but nothing helped. I was being swallowed up by my own sadness and anxiety.

That afternoon, our house filled up with people. Friends came from as far away as Boston. They brought pizza, sandwiches, cookies, cakes, and drinks. Being surrounded by the people I'd felt safest with made me realize that my sense of security had been completely breached. I couldn't bear to think about anyone leaving. How was I going to block the noise in my head once they were gone? How would I distract myself from my troubled thoughts? It was all I could do to take one step after another and breathe.

My sleep that night was fitful and plagued by gnawing thoughts. *Why us?* I wondered, as I lay awake, listening for noises, afraid of what I might hear. *Why defenseless babies? Why my wonderful coworkers, people whose chosen purpose was to guide a community of children to be their best? How will my students carry the burden of what they witnessed?*

Will we ever heal?

December 16, 2012

On Sunday, the superintendent held a private meeting. The e-mail invitation said it was voluntary attendance and for Sandy Hook staff and their families only. I told Nick I wanted to go, to be with friends and colleagues who I knew were struggling as I was. I thought it would be good for all of us to be with one another, to hug, and talk, and cry together for the first time since the worst day of our lives. If I could comfort others, I wanted to be there for them, and I'd hoped their presence would reassure me.

Nick offered to take me. The meeting was held at the Reed Intermediate School, a short distance from our school. When we arrived at the school, the parking lot was already full, so we had to find a space a good distance away. It had taken every ounce of courage I had to even make the drive to Newtown. I was trembling with fear. I imagined threats in every car and on every corner. I wasn't sure I could take the walk from the car to the school. With every step, my heart pounded a little harder. I scanned the landscape around us, watching for bad guys to jump out of the bushes, constantly looking back to see if we were being followed.

This is a mistake, I thought. *I shouldn't have come. I need to go back home.*

Nick held a protective arm around me, urging my every step forward. Finally, we reached the school. I wished there were police officers standing guard, but there were none. We headed to the school library, where the meeting was being held. It was already a full house. I was relieved to see that most of the staff had shown up. The e-mail had said that following the meeting, a bus would take us all to the high school where President Obama was scheduled to speak later that day. Even though it was the president, I couldn't bear the thought of going. The whole town had been invited, and the idea of being in a crowd that size sent waves of panic through my body. I just wanted to grieve with my fellow teachers and go back home.

As we walked in, I hugged some of my colleagues and Nick and I took our seats. A moment later, the superintendent walked in with a group of people I didn't recognize.

When she spoke, she introduced them as a team of mental health experts from Yale. They were there to talk to us about how to proceed when we returned to school. Children are resilient, she said. The sooner they were back in their routine, the better for them. We could have the day tomorrow, she said, and if we wanted to attend any of the twenty-six memorials, the district would provide substitutes for our classes. But school would officially resume on Tuesday.

Tuesday? I tried to process what she said. She was giving us a day to breathe. Then we were all going back to school, and God knows where. And I was expected to leave my students with a substitute, a stranger, after what they'd just been through? Where was the compassion or empathy for our grieving community? The superintendent was telling us, two days after a tragedy of epic proportions, that it was time for us to get back to the classroom and for our students to be back in school. My body shook uncontrollably and I bit my tongue to keep from lashing out, from saying what was on my mind.

We're going back to school on Tuesday? Where are we going back to school? How can anyone possibly think our kids are ready to get back to their "routine" after what they've just experienced? I'm a grown woman and I'm falling apart. I could barely make myself leave my house today. Perhaps if you'd been there you'd understand. How callous and insensitive, I thought. *Twenty-six of us were savagely killed. My students and I barely escaped. Is this how much their lives are valued? Our lives are valued?*

My blood boiled and I couldn't stay quiet anymore. "Excuse me," I said, raising my hand and speaking through gritted teeth. "This is my fiancé who is here with me. His boss has told him he can take an indefinite amount of time off to be with me because I'm too afraid to be alone." *Because his boss understands the magnitude of what has happened here,* I thought. His boss understands that, at this dreadful moment in our community, the right thing to do is comfort our loved ones and one another. But here, where everyone has lost so much, no one seems to understand that. "You expect my students and me to be back—to get back into a routine—on Tuesday?" I asked.

"Absolutely not!" I said.

Grabbing Nick's hand, I turned and walked out of the library, and out of the school.

In the days that followed, I learned that many of my colleagues felt as I did. That we just weren't ready to go back. I don't know exactly what happened after I left the meeting, but some of my colleagues emailed and texted to let me know that our return date had been extended through the holiday break.

Months later, a union representative came forward to say

publicly that neither the teachers nor students had been emotionally prepared to return to school so soon, and that asking us to do so had been a mistake.

The superintendent had become the target of feelings I didn't know what to do with. I'd spat out some of my emotional turmoil at the first person that gave me provocation, but what had I accomplished?

She hadn't been in our school when it was under siege. She hadn't witnessed the frozen faces of sweet little first-graders who thought they were looking at the last moments of their lives. She hadn't heard the sounds my students heard. How could she know how to manage such a horrific tragedy? After all, there was no precedent to follow, no model in place for how to recover from a mass murder at an elementary school.

Who would know the right way to handle that?

Amazing Grace

As afraid as I was to leave my house, I felt I owed it to my courageous colleagues and the beautiful children we lost to dig deep for enough strength to pay my respects and say my good-byes. I'd planned to attend all twenty-six memorials. Tuesday was the first service, the wake for the teacher whose classroom adjoined ours, Miss Soto. We'd often open the door that connected our classrooms to ask quick questions or share supplies. She was an extraordinary young teacher. Everyone thought highly of her (including me), which was evident at the wake.

The funeral home was overflowing with mourners, and as I made my way through the crowd I caught a glimpse of her casket at the front of the room. *How can she be in there?* I asked myself, choking up. *How is that fair? How did this hap-*

pen? I couldn't move. It almost felt as if my feet had melted into the ground. My hands shook and my face flooded with tears and I couldn't catch my breath. I wasn't even able to compose myself with her family members. I knew I had to leave. I couldn't possibly have been helping her loved ones, who were already in such terrible pain. I felt like I was a reminder of how unfair it was that she was gone, because I was alive and there.

Leaving the funeral home, I decided I would not attend any of the other memorial services. The idea of not being able to pay my respects to the others was devastating, but my presence wouldn't be of help to anyone. I retreated back to the refuge of my own home, heartbroken, guilty, and with such a heavy heart that I couldn't even say good-bye the way I wanted to.

After that, my family and friends began building a protective cocoon around me. I was paralyzed by fear and melancholy and shuddered at the thought of going out in public. The world was a scary place and I couldn't imagine it ever feeling safe again. I couldn't even drive to the store to pick up groceries. So loved ones came to me.

My closest friend, Casey, and her husband, DJ, surprised Nick and I one evening with a Christmas tree, complete with ornaments and garland and lights. They played Christmas music and decorated the tree while I sat on the couch and watched forlornly.

Another friend dropped everything on Christmas Eve to stay with me and help me wrap gifts while Nick finally got away to do his shopping.

People called and texted and e-mailed. They picked up groceries and dropped off meals. When Nick ran errands, someone was always there to "babysit" me until he returned. I couldn't stay home alone. Most times I couldn't stand to even be in a room by myself. I whiled away hours watching movies to avoid the news. The endless coverage of the shooter sickened me, and I couldn't bear to see the pain on the faces of the parents who had lost their children, although I certainly admired their courage for speaking out. In those early days, I desperately wished for courage. The courage to walk into a grocery store. To close the bathroom door. To sleep in a darkened room.

My thoughts haunted me. Why wasn't I stronger? What had happened to me? On December 13 I was strong, independent. I had a purpose. Now I was afraid of everything. I felt useless. How would I be able to help my students when I couldn't help myself? They were suffering as I was. They were having problems sleeping. They didn't want to be alone. They were afraid of their own shadows. Would they ever be carefree first-graders again? I wondered. Had their childlike innocence been taken forever? Because we survived, people said we were lucky to be alive. I took that to mean we weren't entitled to grieve. Were we all supposed to just get on with it? To thank our lucky stars that we were still here? Did we even have a right to our pain? I had a million questions and not a single answer.

My friends tried to help me by talking about anything to get my mind off the shooting. Small talk worked for only so long, and then my mind had its way with me again and I was back in that tiny bathroom, listening desperately to the cries of the people who were being hurt, praying for mercy for my students and me. As kind as everyone was being, as much as they did to try to help me work through the quagmire of emotions I was feeling, I wasn't comfortable in my own skin. I slept with the lights on and the TV flickering. I showered with the bathroom door open (still do) because our bathroom doesn't have a window and I feared being trapped. I was afraid of every sound, every stranger, every knock on my door. I dreaded nighttime, when Nick was sleeping and I was alone with my thoughts. When I had nightmares, they sometimes awakened me with loud cracks of gunfire. The life I loved had turned to dark and I feared I would never see light again. *How will I recover?* I wondered. *How will I ever get out of this place I'm in?* A place where everything was murky and frightening and wrong.

I pleaded with God to intervene. Prayer has always played a central role in my life. As a little girl, I knelt by the side of my bed and said the same prayer every night: "Lord, please let me get married and have children, and please let my parents be around to see both." I was seven when I prayed to find my lost doll, Jill. I tore my room apart looking for her, and worried that maybe my mom had mistakenly included her in a bag of used clothes and toys we'd donated to the Salvation Army. When I asked Mom, she said she didn't think that Jill had been donated, but she couldn't be absolutely sure she hadn't accidently tossed her in one of the bags. I'd had Jill since I was a baby and I was really worried about what had happened to her. When all else failed, I sat down and wrote God a letter, asking for his help: "Dear Lord, please bring Jill back. She is very important to me. Love, Kaitlin." I hung the note on our front door, and that night, for extra measure, I also said my bedside prayers asking for Jill's return. It took a few days, but I finally found her, tucked behind a corner of my bed. For a seven-year-old, that was proof enough that God had been listening (or reading).

Growing up, I usually prayed in generalities, but when

something particularly troubling was happening in my young life, I'd tailor my prayers to include whatever it was that was going on, whether it was about a spat with a friend or a math lesson I couldn't master. I remember I prayed my entire sixth-grade year for the mean girl in my class to stop bullying me. I was twelve years old, in a new school, and trying to make friends, but that girl picked me out and taunted me every single day. One time, she knocked a book out of my arms and then stepped on it so I couldn't pick it up. When I grabbed her foot to try to move it off my book, she shouted for everyone to hear that I was feeling her leg (insinuating that I was a lesbian). After that, whenever she saw me in class or in the hallway, she called me Feely. Oh! There's Feely! Who's Feely feeling now?" It sounds funny now. But you remember how it was at that age. All you wanted was for everyone to like and accept you. I was devastated by the mean girl's words and said the same prayer every night: "Please, Lord. Let her stop picking on me and please let everyone else like me." The girl called me Feely for the rest of the year, but I felt better knowing that at least God was on it.

As an adult, I'd strayed from organized religion, but my belief in God and the power of prayer never wavered. I believed in this Bible verse that talks about prayer: "Don't worry about anything; instead, pray about everything. Tell

God what you need, and thank him for all he has done."
I prayed every morning and every night. After the tragedy, I
prayed four and five times a day. I prayed for the twenty-six
people we lost. I prayed for everyone who knew and loved
each one of them. I prayed for our school. I prayed for the
strength to be able to carry the heavy burden of grief I felt. I
prayed for salvation, and the courage to be able to be home
alone, and sleep in the dark, and stop being so afraid. I
prayed that my students and I really had gotten out of that
bathroom alive, and that I wouldn't suddenly wake up from
a nightmare to realize that I hadn't been able to save them
and we were all dead. I thanked him for hearing my prayers.
It was no use.

The only thing that gave me brief moments of solace was
when I was singing "Amazing Grace," the famous folk hymn
and African American spiritual. I'd learned it in church as a
little girl and always found it comforting. Now it was becoming my lifeline. I'd started singing it on the first morning after the shooting. The moment I woke up and my feet
touched the floor, it came to me. At first I hummed it. Later,
I sang the words, sometimes softly, sometimes to myself.

Amazing grace, how sweet the sound,
That saved a wretch like me.

I once was lost but now am found,
Was blind, but now I see.
'Twas grace that taught my heart to fear.
And grace, my fears relieved.
How precious did that grace appear
The hour I first believed.

The lyrics resonated with me. It was comforting to think that someone who was once lost was found, that someone who was blind could see. Perhaps there was hope for me. Hope that one day I would again be the independent woman I once was. A woman who took charge of her life, who was in control of her feelings and emotions, who lived her dreams. But how would I ever be that woman again when the thought of performing the simplest tasks made me freeze? Getting on an airplane. Going to a shopping mall. Walking back into the classroom. It just didn't seem possible that I would ever be able to conquer the fear that was suffocating me—except when I thought about those lyrics. They helped me to breathe. I was once lost, but now I'm found. When I was at my lowest, they sustained me, if only momentarily. In a world that seemed so suddenly dark, that song provided a glimmer of hope. But now I'm found. But now I see. I needed to believe that I, too, could overcome. So I'd sing and sing until I finally fell still. Except that when I stopped singing, the turmoil started all over again. "God," I prayed, "please save me from this bottomless pit of despair."

So it went for days, then weeks.

I don't want to live this way, I thought. *This isn't living. This is a living hell.*

I have to find a way out.

Am I Really Here?

I was able to visit with my students in the week after the shooting. Our room mom invited all of us to her home to make the gingerbread houses we were supposed to make in school that week. Being with my class allowed me—and, I believe, them—a welcome respite from our despair. I knew my students were suffering. It broke my heart to think about first-graders burdened by memories that would paralyze most adults. I thought I'd scream if I heard one more person refer to children as "resilient," inferring that they'd bounce back quickly and with relative ease. If you're talking about recovering from normal childhood setbacks, children are generally pretty adaptable, yes, resilient. But I didn't know of a paradigm for first-graders who lived through what ours had. At least at our room mom's house, my students and I were able to allay our anguish for the few hours we were together. If only it could have lasted.

Almost every day, I had those moments when I asked myself, *Am I really here? Did my students and I really survive? Were we shot and killed like the others, and is this some parallel universe I'm living in? Maybe heaven means everyone knows I've passed except me?* I asked my mom the same questions relentlessly. She patiently assured me that yes, we all got out of the bathroom safely. We were all alive and I was really there, in the present, with her. Her reassurances satisfied me for a little while, but then I'd start doubting again and ask Nick or a friend the same set of questions. "Are you sure my students are alive? Can you prove I'm really here with you?"

I heard from parents that my students were struggling with similar repercussions. Some of them were in treatment for trauma-related stress. Some were plagued by vivid, terrifying nightmares and intrusive thoughts. Others spiraled into panic from sudden sounds: a loud clap of thunder, a slamming door, a police siren. Their wholesome first-grade way of thinking had become infected with the harsh reality that the world could be a very scary place. I often heard about students who were experiencing "irrational fears," for instance, they were terrified that the bad guys were going to return. That didn't sound unreasonable to me. Before the tragedy, worrying that a gunman would go on a murderous rampage in our suburban elementary school would surely have seemed like an "irrational fear."

Our kids were no longer like other kids. Their childhood normalcy had been stolen from them. How do you reassure a first-grader that the monster under their bed isn't real when they've met the monster? How do you tell a child that it's okay to go back to sleep, because it was just a bad dream, when they've lived a nightmare? How do you soften a six-year-old's fear of death when they've seen hell? How in God's name do you help a little one put into any kind of perspective the horror that took place in our school?

I think when you survive a catastrophic event in which so many others have lost their lives and you can't fathom how you didn't, it's hard to grasp that you're still here. You're caught up in a roil of emotion you don't understand. You can feel grateful but still guilty that you survived. You want to appreciate life, but fresh memories of sights and sounds that no one should ever hear or see keep you trapped in a living hell. You need to express your suffering, but you feel unworthy because, after all, you are still alive. I didn't know what to do with all of that turmoil, so how in the world could a first-grader be expected to cope?

I worried that the community—and not in any way out of cruelty or malice, but from a lack of understanding—might not appreciate the intensity of what we'd experienced or the seriousness of the fallout from it. I understood the collective thinking: You are the lucky ones. You survived. But it just wasn't that black-and-white. We had been gravely injured emotionally and we needed time and help to heal.

I desperately wanted my independence again, to get back to the point where I was in control of my emotions rather than my emotions controlling me, to reclaim my lost self. I lived twenty-nine years with the passion and purpose to teach children, to enable their success, and I wanted to be that person again. I just didn't know how. So how would I help my students?

After about two and a half weeks, I knew I couldn't keep going the way I was. I was stuck on a path to nowhere, with no sense of how to get off. Perhaps someone else could guide me in another direction. But who? I wondered. All I knew for sure was that something had to happen if I were to save myself.

My mom was the first person to suggest that I see a therapist. Without my knowledge, she and my best friend Casey were talking regularly by phone about the state I was in and how they might help me. When Mom said she'd already made an appointment for me with a well-respected trauma therapist in the area, I didn't resist. I knew I needed help.

My first appointment with the therapist was at the end of

December. Nick accompanied me to her office. We arrived a few minutes early and signed in at the front desk. A security officer directed us to an office on the first floor. We walked in and Dr. Purcell greeted us warmly. "Please, come in," she said, smiling. I liked her right away. Her poise and self-assurance gave me confidence that maybe she really could guide me back to the Kaitlin I was before. Nick and I sat next to each other on her couch.

"Does it lock?" I asked, glancing at her office door.

"I don't know," she said. "No one has ever asked me that before. I'll check." She disappeared for a minute and then returned with a key, locking us in. "Kaitlin," she said, "I need to let you know that you're safe here. You don't need to be afraid."

For the next hour, I told Dr. Purcell everything from the day of the tragedy. The crackle of gunfire. The shattering glass. The desperate search for someplace to hide. Jamming my kids into an impossibly tiny bathroom. Trying to keep them quiet and calm, knowing that the killer was just a few steps away. Hearing those awful sounds of cornered people pleading for mercy. Waiting for what seemed an interminable amount of time, expecting that at any moment the gunman would discover us and we all would die. As difficult as it was, revisiting what had happened, I found my words spilling out. Dr. Purcell was visibly moved hearing about what my students and I endured. "You were so brave," she said. "You acted so quickly. You saved your students' lives."

It was hard for me to admit my thoughts, which sometimes sounded crazy, even to me, but if I didn't tell my therapist, how could she help me? Toward the end of the session, I confessed that I sometimes questioned the validity of my own story. I'd asked myself, "How did we all fit in that bathroom? We couldn't have, so we must not have. I must be imagining it. How did I pull that cabinet in front of the door? There had been another smaller bookcase next to it. How did I get it out of my way? It doesn't seem possible."

"But you did do those things," she said. "That's why you and your students are still here."

"It's hard to believe I'm here," I said, weighing my words. "Sometimes I don't think I really am. Sometimes I think that I'm really dead and that this is some other place—maybe even heaven."

Dr. Purcell didn't flinch. "You're alive," she said, her eyes soft and kind. "I'm looking right at you. And, yes, your kids made it out of the school."

The time passed so quickly and there was so much I still had to say. I made a second appointment for later that week, determined to do whatever it took to be able to feel normal again. Nick came with me for my second appointment and the one after that. Each time, the therapist and I revisited the same theme. How did I know my students and I were alive? "How do I know you're real?" I asked. Dr. Purcell spent hours patiently reassuring me that everything I was seeing and feeling was actual and authentic. Her reassurances helped me to feel calmer for a while, but I couldn't shake the feeling that I might be dead and, even worse, I hadn't been able to save my students and they, too, were gone. Had I seen them shot? I wondered. Is that why I couldn't remember?

After several sessions, when I still couldn't be convinced that we were all alive, Dr. Purcell took a different tack. "Kaitlin, look," she said, finally. "Just think about this: You keep asking if you're in heaven, but heaven is nothing but good and peace and happiness. You're afraid of everything, so how can this be heaven?" What she said really resonated with me.

I had grown up believing that heaven was a reward, that if you were a good person and lived your life in the service of God you got to go there when you die. If my faith was as strong as I believed it was, she had to be right. There was no suffering in heaven. "Yes," I said. "That makes sense. This can't possibly be heaven. Heaven wouldn't feel this way." It was the last time I asked.

From then on, my therapy focused on preparing me to go

---

back to work. Classes were scheduled to resume on January 3 in a refurbished school building about seven miles from Sandy Hook, in the neighboring town of Monroe. The school had been closed for two years, but was cleaned, painted, and renamed Sandy Hook Elementary during the three-week recess.

The staff was invited for an early visit to the school to survey our new classrooms and get everything in order. I was more interested in safety than furniture and paint. Looking around my room, I saw right away that there was no place to hide. No tiny bathroom. No closets. And the windows were too high to jump from, even if we had the chance to escape. I decided, right then, that before our first day back I had to come up with a safety plan. My students needed to know that, should there be an emergency, we had a blueprint for how to get away.

I took up the issue with my therapist during my next visit with her. "My students are very aware that the only way we survived is because we had a place to hide," I said. "That's the first thing they'll see when they come back—that there's no hiding place. I need a plan." Dr. Purcell agreed a plan was necessary, and we went to work devising a list of ways my students and I could feel confident in our new surroundings.

The plan required asking the administration to provide a few things. First, a new classroom door, because the old one had an oblong glass panel alongside it that someone could easily break to access the lock. Then, a fireman's type of rung ladder, which we could hang from our window and use as a get away if we had to. Third, metal grates installed on the glass windows on either side of the school's main entrance (which were similar to the windows that had been shot out so the shooter could get into our school). And, last, a security guard at the back of the school, at least for the first couple months, and a mental health professional in the classroom to guide me in helping my students reacclimate to the classroom and learn coping mechanisms to deal with their distress.

Having the safety plan gave me the confidence I needed to return to the classroom. I needed to get back, to begin to conquer my own fears and to help my students to overcome theirs, so that one day they could return to being the happy-go-lucky children they deserved to be.

I thought I was ready.

Back to School

I went back to school with a clash of emotions. The thought of returning to class with my students felt absolutely right, but the crater of emptiness left by those who were missing was breathtaking. With the new school came poignant reminders of what once was. There was no happy banter with our beloved principal at the front door, only two uniformed police officers and reverential silence. No joyful sounds of children from the neighboring classroom, just an empty place where they should have been. It all felt surreal. Awful. Terrible. Wrong. Sickening.

At the same time, the distance from what happened gave my students and me a sense of separation from the tragedy. In some way, it felt like a new chance. The district had done a nice job of replicating our classroom in the new school.

Our desks and cubbies, books and toys from Sandy Hook had been moved to our new room before classes started up. Someone had even hung up the jackets the students had left in their haste to get out of our old school.

At 8:55 a.m., like always, my students filed in, as excited to see me as I was to see them. I put on my best face, determined to make the day as comfortable as I could for my kids. I'm not sure what I was expecting, but within minutes I could feel an energy change from our old classroom, a change resulting from the hell my students had been through. Because their trust and sense of security had been shattered, it almost felt as if we were strangers at the beginning of the school year who were just getting to know one another. I knew I had my work cut out for me.

My mom was a huge help. I was asked, prior to the restart of school, if I wanted a guest teacher to assist me through the end of the school year, but I'd declined because it felt like another unwelcome change. Still, I realized that I needed an extra set of hands. My students were in a strange school and didn't know their way around, and I couldn't leave them alone in the classroom to walk someone to the nurse, or the lunchroom, or the lavatory. I had asked my mom if she'd be willing to help and she kindly agreed. She was a reassuring presence, for me and for my students, as were the parents who came in and out to support their children.

That first day, I decided I'd dive right in and pick up where we'd left off a month earlier. For the sake of familiarity, I wanted to stick to our former routine—announcements, attendance, reciting the Pledge of Allegiance. When it came time for morning meeting, we all sat in a circle and I could feel the tension begin to ease.

"Good morning, Fantastic Friends!" I said in my perkiest voice.

"Good morning, Miss Roig," they responded in unison.

First-graders are people pleasers, and mine were trying so hard to be "normal" for me and for one another that my heart broke for them. I was grateful for their sweet smiles, but I saw adult-sized sorrow in their eyes. I wanted to sweep each one of them up in a big bear hug and tell them it was okay to be sad and afraid, that I was, too. But it was my job to stay upbeat and optimistic and allow them to just be children again, at least until they asked for more. That was the one thing I was afraid of: that one of them would ask something I couldn't answer. For instance, Why? Why did this happen? Why did that man do what he did?

Those early days played out in fits and starts. I quickly discovered that, in many ways, it was as if we were back at the beginning of the school year. We were in a brand-new space, and even though the district had done its best to make sure our classroom looked the same, everything was different. My students had to relearn all the things they'd known before the tragedy, from how to carry scissors in the classroom to where to return their supplies and how to organize their desks. It was clear they were suffering, but they weren't able to verbalize their thoughts. A first-grader's ability to articulate feelings is so different from an adult's. It wasn't like dealing with someone who was more mature and could tell you, "I lost my best friend," or, "That was the boy I played with every day." First-graders typically don't express their feelings with words, but their affect told me everything I needed to know. They were generally more introverted, more cautious, quieter. I noticed that the shy students, who had come out of their shells before the shooting, were once again too timid to even raise their hands. I knew it was because they were trembling inside. How could they not have been? I certainly was.

The biggest obstacle I faced was trying to teach around my students' limited attention spans. Or nonexistent attention spans, I should say. They were so anxious and out of sorts that when I was giving a lesson, I'd look out over the class and find that I'd lost half of them before I really got started. Rather than being engaged in the lessons, which they were before the tragedy, now they were "checking out," yawning and squirming and whispering to their neighbors. I'd see them looking up at the ceiling or staring off into space or fidgeting with their hands in their laps. They were always asking for permission to get up to go to the bathroom, or to get a tissue or a drink. Lessons I usually taught in one session were taking three and four. We worked at a slower pace, and I still wasn't sure I was getting through to them.

Every class was interrupted when at least one student, and usually three or four, had a breakdown after hearing an unfamiliar noise coming from upstairs, or the hallway, or the parking lot, and understandably so. When we first got to the new school, we were unaware that construction work was being done in the classroom above ours. The sound of someone dragging a box across the floor upstairs was enough to send one little boy into a fetal position. He curled up into himself, shaking and sobbing hysterically. My heart broke as I tried to console him. Of course, I understood the depth of his fear because all of us felt it. When one student broke down, I could usually calm him or her with soft words and a walk down the hallway. When three or four reacted, we stopped what we were doing, dimmed the lights, put on music, and colored or did yoga poses together.

Often I'd read a story, trying to distract them from their fears. So many family members and close family friends had dropped off children's books they thought would be good for such times. The books were about love and compassion and good-heartedness. A favorite was an illustrated book by Jamie Lee Curtis and Laura Cornell, *Tell Me Again About the Night I Was Born* . . . "Tell me again how you and Daddy were curled up like spoons and Daddy was snoring . . . Tell me again how you called Granny and Grandpa right away but they didn't hear the phone because they sleep like logs." I put all the books on a ledge by my whiteboard to remind myself to read at least one each day.

Whenever something—a sound or a sight or a smell—triggered one of my students, I addressed it with the whole class. I'd say, "Okay, friends, we just heard a noise. I heard it, too. It was a desk being pulled across the floor upstairs. I'm doing okay. Are you?"

Sometimes, I'd call down to the office where the police officers were stationed and say, "We heard something and we are a little nervous. Can you please check and report back to us?" They were so compassionate and reassuring. They always got right back to us.

Sharing with my students, letting them see that we were all in this together and everything possible was being done to keep us safe, usually helped to bring them around, at least for a little while. But those discussions inevitably opened up a floodgate of questions.

"Miss Roig, do you remember that scary day?"

"Absolutely! Yes, I do! I remember that scary day very

well. But we're in a new school and we have police officers here as our helpers and they are watching our school for the bad guys."

"Miss Roig, are the bad guys going to come here?"

"That's why the police officers are here, so that can't happen. That's their job, to keep people safe from the bad guys."

"But Miss Roig, what if the bad guys do get in? Where would we hide?"

"I have a plan," I promised my class. "I'll be able to tell you about it soon."

I PRESENTED MY IDEAS to the acting principal during our first week back. I needed a few extra things to give my students the sense of security they needed, I said. The safety precautions the district had taken were prudent. I had heard repeatedly that ours was the safest school in the United States, and I believed it was. But, except for the police presence, our old school had also had a comprehensive safety strategy, and look what happened there. A buzzer and camera system, lockdown procedures and safety drills, and a partnership with local responders were all positive precautionary measures, but none of those things stopped the shooter from getting into Sandy Hook. As my students' protector, I needed to know that everything possible was being done to make them feel safe and secure. They were astutely aware that we'd survived the first time because we had a place to hide and now we didn't have that. If a bad guy were to get into our class, we were sitting ducks. And even the addition of a police presence hadn't been enough to reassure them about that. Bad guys killed police officers, too.

I explained to the principal that I needed to do something to give my students and their parents some confidence that we were safe in our new school. I felt that, in order for them to stop focusing on the possibility of imminent danger, they needed reassurances that would help them to feel more in control. With that in mind, I said, I'd come up with a specialized plan tailored to our special circumstances that I thought might help make everyone feel more secure. I shared with her the list of suggestions that I thought were very doable: a new classroom door, a fireman's ladder, a security guard behind the school, a temporary mental-health professional in the classroom, and metal grates on the windows framing the main entrance. I explained that I believed having those things would help to ease at least some of the anxiety my students and I were feeling, as well as answer the questions being raised by some parents—specifically, what was our classroom safety plan?

The principal listened politely until I had finished making my case. "I don't think it's necessary," she said. I hadn't even considered she might reject my plan out of hand, but I sensed, at that moment, that our conversation was over and the subject was closed. She had plenty to do in the wake of the tragedy, and meeting the special needs of my class didn't seem to be high on her priority list. But it was at the top of mine.

I say the following to illustrate the point. Sandy Hook Elementary was a big place. K–4. Just under five hundred students. A sixty-six-thousand-square-foot rectangle with an outdoor courtyard in the center. That's nearly ten thousand square feet larger than a football field. The school had four main hallways, one for each grade, and, depending on enrollment, each grade had four to seven classes, plus there was an addition on the back we called "the portables," which housed fourth-grade classes. The shooter never got past the first three first-grade classrooms he encountered when he turned left to the corridor just past the main office. Most of the people in school that day were nowhere near that sliver of hallway where the shootings took place. Many may never have even heard the sound of the gunshots, or the horror of how powerful they were.

Of course you didn't have to see the gunman or hear the gunshots to be traumatized by what happened. Just knowing a madman breached your school is enough to send anyone into distress. What I was trying to say, what I was desperate to get across to school officials, was that my students were likely going to be more affected by the tragedy than many others because of what they'd been witness to, and that we, as adults, needed to take whatever extra measures were necessary to help them to feel safe as they acclimated back into school.

When the principal didn't seem to understand the reasons for my concerns, I decided to go to the superintendent with my proposal. My students were in a unique position, I explained. They had been on the front lines of the vicious attack on our school. They came woefully close to losing their young lives. Had we not somehow squeezed into that unlikeliest of hiding spots, that three-by-four-foot bathroom, we would almost certainly have died. They felt the breath of death as the killer darkened our first-grade corridor. They heard the resonance of carnage, the desperate cries of the victims just before they were murdered in cold blood. At six and seven years old, they knew what it was to be in the presence of evil. How many people ever experience what they did? Because I had, I was keenly aware of how extraordinarily fragile they were, how tenuous their sense of well-being was, how frightening the world looked to them. Several times a day some student asked: "Miss Roig, what are we going to do if another bad guy comes to get us?" They asked because they understood that we shouldn't have survived the first time and the odds of us escaping with our lives again, especially with no place to hide, were slim to none.

I appreciated that the district was providing counselors and extra security in our new school, but I thought more could be done to reassure those who had been in close proximity to the massacre. My students needed tangible evidence that everything humanly possible was being done to ensure their safety. At the very least, they needed to know we had a ladder that we could toss out the window and climb down as reassurance that, if we were ever to be faced with a similar situation, which I realized was unlikely, we had some means of escape.

The district was doing enough, the superintendent said.

"I respectfully disagree," I said.

Where do I go from here? I wondered.

CHOOSING TO
OVERCOME

"I have never felt that anything really mattered but the
satisfaction of knowing that you stood for the things
in which you believed, and had done the very best
you could."

—ELEANOR ROOSEVELT

The Questions
I Could Answer

Every day when we walked into our new school we discovered more gifts. They came from people around the world—kind people who wanted to do something to help our community heal. The outpouring was so overwhelming that a town official was charged with overseeing the sorting and cataloging of all the things sent by well-wishers. The numbers were staggering. Hundreds of thousands of cards and letters, toys, and monetary donations poured in.

According to the local newspaper, in that first week alone, town officials inventoried 63,780 teddy bears, 636 boxes of toys, 2,200 boxes of school supplies, as well as bicycles and backpacks and cookies and cupcakes and boxes and boxes of tissues. It took an army of nearly six hundred volunteers just to sort the iTunes and Starbucks gift cards.

My class received stuffed animals in every size and color, and art supplies, and books by the dozens, and our own toy therapy dogs. Knowing we were in others' thoughts and prayers, that complete strangers cared about us and our town, provided a welcome reprieve in what continued to be very challenging times.

My wounded students deserved every moment of happiness they could get. But about two weeks in, as the gifts kept coming, it struck me that perhaps I was missing the opportunity to reinforce a very important life lesson for my first-graders. The lesson that teaches, while it is wonderful to receive, it feels even better to give. So many people had given of themselves to us and I thought it was our social responsibility to pay the kindness forward. We just needed to find a way to do it.

Up to that point, I had continued to obsess over the "Why?" of what happened. The question was always met with silence because, of course, there was no answer, and that had only fueled my anger and frustration. That day, though, I realized I could continue to torture myself by asking the unanswerable, or give myself permission to refocus on questions that could be answered. And I could share that mission with my students. Together we had witnessed great evil and now we were being showered with goodness. In was within our power to choose which to focus on. Even though we couldn't answer why, we could answer things such as: How do we find good after evil? How do we get our control back? How do we persevere in a way that will honor the friends we have lost? The answer was the same to all of the questions: by giving.

"I have found that among its other benefits, giving liberates the soul of the giver," Maya Angelou wrote. Giving was a way to channel our grief, and perhaps even give us the solace we were seeking. By focusing on someone else's needs, rather than our own sadness, the very least that could happen was we would do some good in the world. But who would we help? And how?

For my entire career, I tried to incorporate aspects of a social curriculum into my classwork. Solid test scores and strong scholastic skills are crucial for the success of every student, but teaching youngsters how to interact and empathize with one another, to feel good about themselves and their relationships, and giving them the tools to be socially aware and emotionally intelligent is every bit as important. The foundation of a social curriculum is teaching lessons that lead to a greater good, whether it is in the classroom, or the school, or the community, or the world. *What better lesson than one that teaches the importance of giving?* I thought.

And so one afternoon I brought a large box a friend of mine had mailed to my class and I placed it in front of them.

"This box is filled with **things for** us to use today during recess," I said, pulling out puzzles and games and coloring books and colorful markers. Their eyes grew wide at the prospect of playing with their newest gifts. "Do you know why someone sent this to us?" I asked. Their hands shot up. "Because they wanted us to be happy," one of the students said. "They wanted to be nice," another student said. "They wanted us to have fun at recess," said a third child. "You are all exactly right!" I said. "Someone did this for us, for all of those reasons. In life, when someone does something nice for you, you have to do something nice for someone else, and that is what we are going to do!"

At that point, I had a "lightbulb moment." In first grade, that's what we call it when an idea finally clicks. "I've got it!" I said. "We are going to find a class somewhere in the United States and we are going to make them feel the way we do right now. We're going to make them feel happy."

Now their eyes got even wider with excitement. They were squealing with anticipation. "Who are we going to help?" they asked. "How are we going to help them?" "When are we going to start?"

I marveled at the benevolence of my students. They were more excited at the prospect of giving to others than the gifts they had just received. They got right down to work. For the next week, we focused on the idea of giving. I found short video clips of readings from the PBS children's series *Reading Rainbow* and read them stories from books with giving themes. *Boxes for Katje*, *The Berenstain Bears: Kindness Counts*, and, of course, *The Giving Tree*. That was their favorite.

> "I don't need very much now," said the boy, "just a quiet place to sit and rest. I am very tired."
>
> "Well," said the tree, straightening herself up as much as she could, "well, an old stump is good for sitting and resting. Come, Boy, sit down. Sit down and rest."
>
> "And the boy did. And the tree was happy."

We had daily conversations about the meaning of benevolence and generosity and gratitude and why it was so important to help our fellow man. At the same time, after class, I searched the Internet for ideas on how we might go about developing our project. It had to be an authentic experience, one in which we could connect with the receiving class so my students could see firsthand the impact of their giving.

Around that time, a group from Tennessee visited our school to make a donation and do whatever they could to help the community. One of them was a teacher. I told her about our idea and she gave me the name of a new teacher in her school whose class had many needs.

I contacted that teacher and explained what we wanted to do. Was there something we could do for her class? Something they needed? The teacher responded that at the top of her wish list was an interactive whiteboard, which would allow her to access the Internet on a computer and share it on the whiteboard with the whole class.

The next day, I shared the exciting news that we had a recipient for our giving project. My students were beside themselves with excitement. I showed them the state of Tennessee on the map in our classroom and explained how the whiteboard would help the receiving class with their daily lessons. They got right down to work, drawing handmade cards to go with our gift, which we purchased using donations that had been sent to us. Ours was the first class to reach out to another class and say, "What do you need? How can we help you?"

My students wanted to feel better, and my job as their teacher was to give them the opportunity to turn that terrible tragedy into something positive. When they seized the opportunity—when they chose that glimmer of hope—was when I knew that the shooting was not going to define them or me. I didn't know how long it would take, but I knew we would eventually be okay.

That was a first step on our long path to healing.

Focusing on the Positive

Our community lost its equilibrium after the massacre. The tragedy was so enormous, so incomprehensible, so outside the realm of normality that we were rocked off balance. When your world feels so out of control, you tend to grab what little control you still have. For me, it was my classroom. Throughout January, I continued to advocate for ways to help my students feel safer at school. They still worried about having no place to hide in our classrom. They jumped at every unfamiliar sound. They needed a chaperone (my mom) to take them to the bathroom, or to the office, or anywhere else outside of our classroom, because what if a bad guy was out in the hallway shooting at people again? In many cases, I was the only person a student felt comfortable with besides their parents. The month was almost over and one of my students still refused to come to school without her mother because she felt so vulnerable with no place to take cover in our new room. I couldn't blame her. When the mom went to the administration to inquire about a plan to make her daughter feel safer, she was told, "Miss Roig has good instincts. She will protect the students."

I was unhappy to hear the response. I'd been able to protect my students at Sandy Hook because we at least had a place to get away from the danger. In the new classroom, there was nowhere for us to hide and no way out of our room except for the door leading into the hallway. Going out that way would have meant certain death in our old school. My students knew that. That's why I'd asked for a ladder for the window, as reassurance that we could get away if we had to.

For weeks, I'd been trying to get the superintendent to understand my logic, but all of my suggestions were rejected. I realized that the resistance wasn't about district resources when I told her I'd found someone who was willing to donate and install a new classroom door and she still refused, saying a new door wouldn't meet code or match the other doors in the school. When I wanted to use some of the donations we'd received to purchase the fireman's ladder, she said they were unsafe for small children. But I had to wonder: Less safe than being trapped in a room with no way to evade a madman intent on killing us? I explained that I realized it was unlikely we would ever have to use the ladder, that that wasn't the point. (Of course, if someone had predicted what had already happened to us, we would have called them crazy. And there is the saying that lightning never strikes twice.) It wasn't about the ladder, I said. It was about easing my student's minds.

"We have done everything to make the school safe," she said.

None of it made sense to me. Sometimes it felt as though people just didn't get it, that they had somehow misinterpreted what it was I was trying to do. How could I make them understand that those few relatively minor things would give my students and their parents a little peace of mind? Didn't they deserve that?

I certainly wasn't going to retreat, not when my students were still beleaguered by constant thoughts of a monster that they knew was real. Why wasn't I being trusted to know what was best for them? Why had our needs been repeatedly dismissed with the pronouncement that enough had been done? If that were true, if enough had been done, I wouldn't have had sixteen stressed-out first-graders who were so distracted by fear that they couldn't get through a day without tearful outbursts.

I convinced myself that the superintendent would eventually come around. How could she not? In the meantime, I did my best to focus on positive things that were happening.

I'd never seen my students as happy as they were when they were helping the class in Tennessee to purchase the interactive whiteboard. Seeing those genuine first-grade smiles again was a sight for sore eyes. Our giving project had provided them with a few hours of happiness during an otherwise terrifically demanding time for all of us. Their joy from giving was palpable and, just as I had hoped, the students from Tennessee chose to reciprocate by paying it forward.

I got to thinking. We, as a society, are so driven to accumulate possessions and wealth that we often forget about how good it feels to give, to share our own goodness with others. The act of giving is so powerful. What better example of that than the joy it brought my first-graders, even during a chapter in their lives that was shrouded in deep sorrow and unhappiness? The message had caught on with the class in Tennessee, so why not share it in a bigger way? Why not invite students all over the country to experience the pleasure of giving the way we did? Why not grow a social movement to teach schoolchildren kindness and empathy, not by just talking about it, but by living it, in the way my first-graders had?

After school one night I jotted down some ideas on a slip

of paper. The concept of students giving to students could be featured on a website and work the way our class project had. We had reached out and asked the school in Tennessee what we could do to help them, and then we'd used resources that were donated to us to fulfill their need. The premise of a website could be the same: donors would contribute to the site, and classes could pay for needs posted by other classes using those donations.

I surfed the Web to see if there was anything out there like it, certain that someone was ahead of me, but there was nothing to be found. That gave me the green light to share my idea with other teachers. I called teachers who were friends to solicit their thoughts. During each call I explained the concept and how it might impact the way our students learned to care about one another. I made several calls a night, and everyone I spoke with was really receptive. By the time I was finished making calls, fourteen teachers were on board and couldn't wait to get started, and each had promised to recruit another teacher or sponsor to help get the program off the ground.

At my next therapy session, I shared with Dr. Purcell that I was ready to move in a different direction in my healing. "Thank you for all of your help," I said. "I appreciate everything you have done for me. I've learned so much. But I truly think that, going forward, my healing needs to be action, doing something." I explained about the nonprofit and the goal of it, "to help children to learn to care by being actively engaged in caring about others," and how working toward something so positive had made me feel better than I had in weeks. "I really think throwing myself into this is my healing," I said. "It makes me feel happy and hopeful and in control again."

Dr. Purcell gave me her blessing. She said she was a firm believer that different people needed different ways to cope with trauma. "Action is healing," she said. That really resonated with me. Having her support was a pivotal moment in my recovery. Her belief in me was the reassurance I needed that I was on my way back from the tragedy and strong enough to travel the rest of the road without her professional guidance. We agreed that would be my last session and promised to stay in touch. When I left her office, I felt lighter. I was going to see to it that something good came from what seemed like an unredeemable tragedy.

That night I wrote in my journal.

In this tragedy, I have been confronted with an outpouring of good, hope, caring, compassion on behalf of the people in our country, which is how this idea came to me. If, after such a horrific event, we are going to choose love, caring, consideration, compassion, empathy, and hope, which I so believe we should, then we need students around our nation to have the opportunity to be a part of something that exhibits all of these. We can teach every child to care for one another by caring for others, and to have genuine interest in others by showing interest in others ourselves, and to be kind by showing them that we practice acts of kindness. We can teach every child to learn how to love by being loving. We can teach them to understand that our lives are not separate, but in fact, completely connected. When we teach kindness, caring and love, then there is no room for hate.

Everything started falling into place really quickly. I was referred to a Web designer and we drafted a mock website together. She and I became fast friends, and I asked if she'd consider being on a board of directors and she excitedly agreed. Two local businessmen, both with nonprofit experience, also accepted an invitation to join. I felt honored that such experienced and accomplished people were willing to volunteer their time to help grow a concept we all believed in.

Within days of hatching the idea, I had a team of passionate, creative, committed professionals who believed wholeheartedly in the mission. At our first meeting, we drafted ideas for a logo on the back of a coaster and we settled on a name. We would call it "Classes 4 Classes," with a subtitle of "Kids Pay It 4ward." We were on our way.

Around the same time, I received a letter from the principal of the school in Tennessee.

"Dear Kaitlin," she wrote,

> *I just wanted to let you know how thankful I am for the inspiration that you have been to so many people in our school. Our students are super excited about receiving the wonderful gift of a mimeo system. But, even better, the students are so enthusiastic about the opportunity to help others.*
>
> *In addition, one of our parents is talking to the other people in her nursing class, about becoming a caring class, so your idea is spreading to other age groups as well.*
>
> *Although I know that our job as teachers is to prepare our students academically for what lies ahead, I believe that instilling love and caring for others is an even greater obligation.*
>
> *Thank you for the opportunity to do this.*

I returned to school with renewed energy and my therapist's mantra: "Action is healing."

Standing for What's Right

My diary of what happened next is something I have never shared. I do so here with mixed emotions, but for the sole reason that I believe good comes from truth. Someone, somewhere, will benefit from it. Perhaps by thinking twice before rejecting outright the suggestion of another. Perhaps by being more open and inclusive when making a decision that affects many. Perhaps by being reminded of the importance of humility and respect, and how everyone is entitled to be treated with kindness and consideration.

My hope is that telling this truth will also set me free from the judgments of those who assumed they knew the circumstances of the conflict with our superintendent, but really had no idea what took place. Free from the hurtful words of critics who condemned me for abandoning my students when I did not abandon them. Anyone who knows me knows I never would.

There's a saying that goes, "Always speak the truth, even if your voice shakes." My voice is shaking as I write this.

Toward the end of January, after a month of reiterating my requests for my kids, I was pulled out of my classroom and into a meeting with the superintendent and the director of human resources. I was told that, once and for all, they would not implement my ideas and if I wasn't okay with that, I needed to take a break. I walked away stunned. Our former principal, who had given her life trying to stop the shooter, had a motto: "Be safe, responsible, respectful, and prepared." That's what we lived by at Sandy Hook, and that's what I was trying to convey to my first-graders by asking for things that would allow them to feel more secure in the classroom. I thought I was doing what every good teacher does: advocating for my students. Yet here I was being given an ultimatum: stop asking or leave.

I took a night to think about it, and then called the human resources director to say I wasn't leaving. My students had already been through enough upheaval without losing their teacher, too. "And if I am leaving, you will need to tell the parents of my students that I am going against my will," I said. She said she would get back to me. Later that afternoon, I got the verdict. The superintendent had decided to let me stay.

"Let" me stay?

I was angry. I felt as if I was being treated like a malcontent. I had never been difficult or a complainer. Before the shooting I'd had little to no contact with the superintendent and my relationship with our principal at Sandy Hook had been warm and affable. Now it seemed as if my continued quest for what I believed was best for my first-graders was being interpreted as disobedience. I tried to make sense of it all. After what our community had been through, everyone was dealing with heightened feelings that we didn't quite know what to do with and I was no exception. The magnitude of the tragedy was reflected in the scope of people affected by it and the range of emotions we were experiencing. Triggers were everywhere. People had their own ways of coping, but how could anyone know "the right way" to deal with such an inimitable event and all of its terrible implications? There wasn't a blueprint for how to deal with what we had all been through. I tried to understand the stress the superintendent was under, but I also couldn't help but feel under siege.

Not a week later, a co-teacher was brought into my classroom, despite my earlier decision that I didn't need one. She was a lovely woman and eager to help, but there wasn't much for her to do. My mom and I had things under control and she had been a real comfort to my kids. After the co-teacher had been with us for a few days, I was called to the office and told that she was capable of assisting me with whatever I needed, and my mom would have to pack up her things and leave. I was heartbroken to have to tell my mom. After all she had done for us, no one in the administration even thanked her when she left.

Then came the straw that broke the camel's back. A former professor of mine, Dr. Douglas Kaufman from the master's program at UConn, contacted me and offered to come into my class to conduct a writing program for my students. His idea was to help them write a class book—nothing to do with trauma or tragedy, just a nice kids' story—and maybe even get it published. His thought was that after all that had been taken from the kids, the writing project would give them back a sense of control and a strong feeling of accomplishment. And he offered to do it out of the goodness of his heart. *What an opportunity,* I thought. Dr. Kaufman's credentials were impeccable. In addition to being the associate professor of curriculum and instruction at UConn's Neag School of Education, he had published well-received books about literacy and teaching and teacher-student relationships, and he presented his work at educational conferences around the world. The man was in such demand, and he was offering himself to us for free.

I thought it was a brilliant idea and floated it to a couple parents, who agreed. So I composed a letter to send home with my students. Dated February 19, 2013, it read:

Dear Family,

I am so excited to share with you an amazing opportunity that our class is going to be a part of! My grad school professor Douglas Kaufman reached out to me to see if he could be of service. Dr. Kaufman is involved in the UConn Writing Project, and goes into K-5 classrooms to get kids excited about writing and illustrating. His passion and excitement are truly contagious. I asked him if he would be willing to come in to our classroom to write and illustrate with us, and his answer was "Absolutely!" He is currently on sabbatical, working on his own writing publications. His first day with us will be Tuesday, March 5. He will most likely come two days a week for the duration of a month or so. During this time he and I will be co-teaching and helping the students to harness their ideas into one clear vision. They will be writing a class book. Dr. Kaufman will then

*bring this book to other elementary schools he works with
and share it with them! I just know our class will be so
excited to write and illustrate with Dr. Kaufman. It will
be such a positive experience, to write with an author. If
you have any questions please contact me anytime!*

Before sending the letter, I sent an e-mail to the administration that explained my plan to bring the professor in and
convey how excited we were to begin. When I didn't hear
back, I sent a second e-mail. The vice-principal called me to
her office. No go, she said. The professor wasn't trained in
mental health, so he couldn't come to our class.

My face flushed with incredulity. In my wildest dreams,
I hadn't anticipated that this initiative would be turned
down. "I don't understand why everything I'm asking for for
my students is being denied," I said. "First, ways to make
them feel safe. Now a writing workshop? Which has everything to do with giving them a positive experience?" My
frustration bubbled over and spilled out. "Our old school
and leadership came from a place of 'Yes! Yes, we can,'" I
said. "Now I am living in a world of 'No.'" With that, I
turned and walked out of the office and back to my class.

Shortly afterward, I received notice that I was to report to
a meeting with the superintendent at the board of education
offices on March 5, the same day the writing project would

have begun. I sought the counsel of a union rep, who advised me that, because the superintendent and I were at a standoff, and chances were good that she wouldn't change her mind, I should agree to take a few weeks off to give us both some breathing room and the conflict time to simmer down.

Still, when the meeting came, I walked into it with high hopes. I had to believe the superintendent would finally agree that we needed to do whatever was necessary to help my students to move forward—and the writing project would have been a positive experience that had nothing to do with the tragedy. We greeted each other cordially and she proceeded to once again recite my list of requests. "I'm not giving them to you," she said. "If you're still not okay with it, you need to take a leave." To say I was angry would be to grossly understate my feelings at that moment. My very reasonable requests had been repeatedly met with such an adamant negative response and it didn't make any sense to me. All I could think was that my kids' well-being was being turned into a pretext in a contest of wills. But a contest needs two to compete, so I decided to remove myself right then. My students were too important to me to allow them to get caught in the crosshairs of bureaucracy and I could never agree that they didn't need extra consideration. "Our lives begin to end the day we become silent about the things that matter," Martin Luther King Jr. once said. I knew our needs mattered even if no one else agreed. "I completely disagree with you, but I have to comply," I said.

The conditions of my leave were that I was to stay away until I was ready to accept the superintendent's terms. In the meantime, I was to have no contact with my students. I couldn't even return to my classroom to explain that I would be gone for a few weeks. I never got the chance to say good-bye.

The mother of one of my students wrote me afterward. I have her handwritten note framed on a table in my living room.

Kaitlin,

There are no words to thank you for what you have given us this year. No gift can come close to repaying you or showing you how grateful we are to you for your actions. You will forever be a part of our hearts and we will always remember not just your actions but how hard you fought for our kids. I hope one day you and Nick will have kids and you will understand the enormity of your gift to us.

I wondered if that mom understood the enormity of the gift she had given me.

Going Back

My plan was to be back in the classroom by April 1. I was certain that even though my requests were easily refused, the parents of the students' wishes wouldn't be, and I was certain that they would take up the safety argument where I left off and advocate for my immediate return. Meanwhile, when I contacted Dr. Purcell to tell her what had happened, she was bewildered, and wrote the district a letter on my behalf.

The letter, dated March 21, 2013, said:

Kaitlin Roig sought my professional help following the Newtown massacre.

As is evidenced by her response to this horrific event, Ms. Roig is resilient and reacts with incredible speed and judgment in the face of crisis. She came to see me determined to take all the necessary steps to deal with the trauma she experienced, begin the healing process, and return to her job as a first-grade teacher at Sandy Hook Elementary School.

When one experiences a trauma such as what happened in Newtown (and specifically in Ms. Roig's classroom) the unthinkable has occurred. As a result, what previously felt safe no longer does. In such circumstances, taking specific and concrete actions to further secure the environment is necessary if healing is to occur. For this reason, Ms. Roig and I devised a "safety plan" in preparation for her return to work.

. . . I do not release my patient to return to work until she and her students' needs have been met. Given the magnitude of the trauma, her requests are reasonable and necessary . . . She needs to know that she can work in a reasonably safe environment and can provide the same for her students . . .

After her requests are met we will then be in a position to determine a return to work date for her.

Thank you for your attention to this critical situation.

For the rest of that month, I kept myself busy with preparations for the April launch of the Classes 4 Classes website. I was usually in meetings with our new executive board, or working with our Web designer, writing and rewriting content for the site and making sure all of the parts were in the right place. At least a couple times a week, I traveled to New York City to share our vision for the nonprofit with executives and solicit corporate support. My goal was to set everything in place for the launch before I returned to school in early April, because after that I would need to give my full attention back to my kids.

I heard in various ways that the parents of my students had, indeed, been lobbying for a safer classroom and for my immediate return. Hardly a day went by that I didn't get phone messages, texts, and e-mails asking when I would be back, and offering bits of information about what was being done on my behalf. All of the messages offered a similar sentiment: "We need you back. Our kids need you back." I was so grateful for the dedication and loyalty of my students' parents. We had developed strong relationships from the beginning of the school year, and those ties only got tighter after the tragedy. Their commitment to their children and their support for me was sustaining during those weeks I was away. They had been actively advocating for what was right, just like I had. Other teachers also felt that the district needed to do more to make the students feel safe, but, after seeing the administration's response to me, they decided not to pursue their requests.

The first and second weeks of April came and went with no word. It occurred to me that the district could be running out the clock. Only six weeks remained in the school year. Around that same time, I heard the troubling news that the family of one of my students had endured a personal hardship. *What else would this poor child have to endure?* I wondered. I contacted his mom to say how sorry I was that they were going through such a difficult time, and asked if there was anything I could do to help. She responded immediately that a visit with her son would be beneficial. "He would love to see you," she said. "He's been asking for you. He's been wondering if you're okay." *Of course he was,* I thought. I'd vanished from his life with no explanation because I hadn't been allowed to return to my classroom, not even to say good-bye.

We made arrangements to meet for lunch two days later, on April 13, at the local Friendly's restaurant. The whole family came and we had a wonderful visit. Afterward the mom texted me: "Thank you so much," she wrote. "He has been all smiles and singing since you left. I think just knowing you are REALLY okay is what he needed. He is so happy. Thank you."

I texted back, "I am so glad. That makes me so happy. Please tell him how much I loved having lunch with him."

"Oh, he knows," she responded. "He was so happy that you sat next to him. You are very loved. Stay strong and change for no one. We all love you."

"Means the world to me and I love you all, too," I wrote.

Of course, it occurred to me that the terms of my leave were that I was to have no contact with my class, but that never entered into my decision to have lunch my student and his family that day. A child I cared about was suffering and I needed to be there to support him and his family. But the superintendent didn't see it that way.

In early May, my therapist received her response.

The superintendent was satisfied that the school district had provided the proper safeguards for the students and nothing further needed to be done. When I felt ready, they would be happy to discuss my return to work date.

I received my own letter from the superintendent the same day, letting me know that she had heard about the visit with my student, and reprimanding me for breaking a condition of my leave. Before I could return to my classroom, she wrote, I would need to be evaluated by an independent medical professional.

The superintendent had waited more than a month to respond to the matter of my reinstatement, and she'd done it one day before leaving the district. I was aware that, months before the shooting, a majority of the board of education had voted against extending her three-year contract, but I had no idea she'd decided to leave early to take a job in a nearby town. I read about it in the local newspaper and I was stunned. That week was "the official end of her stormy five-year employment in town," the story in the *NewsTimes* in Danbury said.

The letter to me was one of her last acts as our superintendent. I read and reread it, probably four or five times. The way I interpreted it, the issue had gone from a disagreement over safety to a question of whether I was fit to return to the classroom. The findings of my therapist, who had more than twenty years of experience in her field, were dismissed and my advocacy was being painted as instability. Why was my character and mental health called into question when neither had ever been an issue before? All too aware that the school year was winding to a close, and anxious to get back to my students, I tossed the letter on the table and began searching for, as was requested, "a medical professional to ascertain that I was able to return to my teaching duties." I decided to seek two opinions and made appointments for the following week. Both did evaluations and passed me with flying colors. To sum up their findings: I was not suffering from post-traumatic stress disorder. I was acting with prudence and in the best interest of my students. I was perfectly fit to return to school.

"[Kaitlin] is an extraordinarily resourceful, competent woman, who not only uses her cognitive and interpersonal tools to handle any stressors, but also has been able to move forward, making admirable progress professionally and personally from her experience," one wrote. "She is fully ready to resume her active teaching duties . . . It would also greatly benefit the children in her class to have her return. After what Ms. Roig and the children experienced on Dec. 14th, she is obviously a very important person in their and their families' lives."

I appreciated the vote of confidence, but it came too late for me. By the time the evaluations had been completed and the recommendation letters written, school was almost over. Rather than working together to come up with even a compromise, to do whatever was best for sixteen first-graders, the dispute had become a battle of wills and, in my mind, everyone lost. Especially my kids.

My heart broke when I read the cards and letters they sent.

Miss Roig, I love you. You are the best teacher in the world. I wish you came back on Monday.

Miss Roig, I miss you. A lot! When are you going to come back?

Miss Roig, I love you and we want you back, so, so much!

Newtown was suffering from gaping psychological wounds that would likely take years to heal, and all of us were still in the early stages of our recovery. We were living the "disaster after the disaster," where nothing was normal and no one knew how to dig out from under the collective sadness and anger and disappointment that blanketed our community. The initial sense of togetherness was cracking, as was to be expected, and everyone was coping with their grief in different ways. Discontent always lay just under the surface and sometimes those simmering feelings of helplessness and inadequacy to make things better led to conflicts with each other.

My spirit was wounded by the superintendent's attack on my character and, in spite of myself, I felt anger and resentment toward her.

Then, one night, as I was searching for inspiration in the words of great orators, I found a quote by Dr. Martin Luther King Jr.: "Darkness cannot drive out darkness: only light can do that," he said. "Hate cannot drive out hate: only love can do that." His words really resounded with me. If Dr. King could choose optimism over adversity after all the disappointments and setbacks that he faced in his lifetime, then who was I to carry bitterness and blame?

I thought about my conflict with the superintendent differently after that. I couldn't help but wonder if both of us had taken some of our pent-up feelings of anger and frustration over the tragedy out on each other. The intensity of my indignation subsided and I tried to see things from her perspective. Perhaps, in her mind, she was doing what she had to do. How many people have had to live through what we just did? Who knew the right way to cope with the fallout from the kind of trauma most people never experience? I'm sure she spent every day like the rest of us did—just trying to get through it. Perhaps she was disappointed after not being reinstated and I had been an easy target for her anger. Perhaps we were both being willful because it was easier than facing what we were really feeling: powerlessness.

Whatever it was, what became clear to me was that I didn't have room in my heart for darkness or hate. I needed to choose light. And love.

My Kids

On a perfect, sunny Saturday afternoon in June, I was reunited with my first-graders at a reunion party my room moms put together at one of their homes. Driving there, I felt like a kid on Christmas Eve. I couldn't wait to see my little angels again. Snips and snails and puppy-dog tails. Sugar and spice and everything nice. That's what my kids were made of. I longed to see their bright eyes, hear their tinkling giggles.

Arriving at the party, I felt as if I was reentering the world we'd lost the previous December, a world I had longed to return to but feared it no longer existed. As Nick and I walked to the backyard, where all of my students were waiting for me, there it was again, right in front of me. I watched in awe as my sweet first-graders, all of them dressed in bright summer colors, ran barefoot through the grass and splashed in the kiddie pool. They looked so carefree. Every night, I'd prayed for them to be able to be happy-go-lucky kids again. *Prayers answered*, I thought, walking toward them.

They squealed when they saw me, stopped whatever they were doing, and ran to us. "Miss Roig!" "Miss Roig is here!" "Miss Roig, I'm so happy you're okay!" Oh, those beautiful toothless smiles! Those funny little cowlicks! Those little fingers painted in varying shades of girlish pink. Stretching and straining their little arms, and clamoring to get as close as they could, my students surrounded me for a big, group hug. How do I describe what I felt? The last time we were huddled so closely together was in the classroom bathroom. For the briefest moment, my mind went back there, and I worried that some of them were thinking the same thing. *But we aren't in that tiny bathroom*, I told myself. *We are here, in this safe place, and blessed to be all together again. This is a time for rejoicing. There is no place, on this beautiful day, with these precious children, for looking back.* We needed to allow ourselves this moment, however brief, to bask in feelings of gratitude that we were together again. Today, we would be "our class," just the way we were before everything changed. "Hello, my Fantastic Friends!" I said, spreading my arms as far as they would reach around my kids. "I'm so happy to see you!"

For the rest of the afternoon, we had a party. We pushed one another on the swings and played dodge ball and catch until we were too tired to move. We snacked on chips and pretzels and Popsicles and fruit and juice. I brought the Crumbs cupcakes for dessert. I'd started a tradition of bringing the gourmet cupcakes to class for special occasions, and my students loved them.

I hated to see the day end. But as the party wound down, my students sat in a circle around me and presented me with a beautifully wrapped box. I slowly pulled the wrapping off the gift to reveal the most beautiful handmade platter with thumbprints painted like bumblebees. Beneath each of the thumbprints was a student's name. The back of the platter was inscribed: "Ms. Roig. 2013. You have left an imprint on our lives."

I was so touched. I couldn't imagine they would ever understand just how deep an impression they had left on my life. I always felt a sense of loss when my first-graders moved on, but leaving these students was going to be especially hard. We had been through something together that no one else could possibly understand, and through that, we had forged an unbreakable bond.

As I told them in the classroom bathroom that day, "I love you all very much." And I truly did.

My Friends, the Authors

B efore I left the party with my class, they had one more surprise. Our dream after the tragedy had been to write that book together, the one my former professor offered to help with, the happy keepsake that we could take out at any time to remember one another and smile. I'd given up on the idea after everything that happened with the superintendent, but my students hadn't. They presented me with a beautiful bound book. They chose the topic themselves and each contributed to it. Our room moms helped them to put it all together. The book cover has a classic white cover with black lettering and is professionally bound. It has sixteen pages, one for each student, and is titled, *All of the Things We Love About Miss Roig*, along with the following message to my 2012 first-grade class:

My Friends, the Authors

Dear Fantastic Friends! After the tragedy, I promised you that we would publish a book about whatever topic you chose. Here is your book. This is your idea and these are your words, and I am bursting with pride to be able to share them here. You should be so proud! You are now published authors!

It is with great pride that I deliver on my promise to my students and share here their words:

ALL OF THE THINGS WE LOVE ABOUT MISS ROIG

By: Miss Roig's 2012–2013 First-Grade Class

This year Miss Roig taught me to read chapter books.

This year Miss Roig taught me where to put capital letters and punctuation.

Miss Roig loves me because she kept me safe. I love Miss Roig because she kept me safe.

What I will miss most about Miss Roig is that she's a wonderful person and that she inspires me.

I love Miss Roig because she has great hair.

I love Miss Roig because she is a hero and kind. This year Miss Roig taught me that even though bad things happen, it will be okay.

Miss Roig loves me because I am a good student.

This year Miss Roig taught me how to read. And now I love to read!

~

This year Miss Roig taught me tricky word tricks in reading.

~

What I will miss most about Miss Roig is . . . I don't want to do "miss." It makes me sad.

~

What I will never forget about Miss Roig is that she is very nice and sweet.

~

What I will miss most about Miss Roig is that she made me feel loved. I love Miss Roig because she is nice and protective. This year Miss Roig taught me how to spell "bed" using my hands.

~

What I will never forget about Miss Roig is that she likes books that won the Caldecott awards. And almost every day she wore a fleece jacket.
    She really cares about us. Because of all of the things she did.

~

I really want Miss Roig back from vacation.

~

What I will never forget about Miss Roig is that she taught us poems.

The sixteenth page is blank.

My student had missed me so much that she'd been too upset to write, her father told me.

When I saw her at the party, she ran to me and hugged me so tightly I could hardly breathe. She just needed to know that I was okay and hadn't abandoned her.

What I will never forget about that little girl is the look in her eyes. It was pure joy.

CHOOSING
YOUR PATH

"What you do makes a difference, and you have to decide what kind of difference you want to make."

—JANE GOODALL

Classes 4 Classes

I am an ordinary person who persevered after what, had I decided, could have been an insurmountable tragedy. And, through that, I realized that some of our most powerful lessons come from being faced with adversity. If only we're open to receiving those lessons. We have so much more power over our lives than we think we do. We all suffer at times. We all experience disappointments and sadness and hard times. We all have tragedies in our lives. It is how we decide to handle our trials that distinguish us. Anne Frank wisely wrote, "How wonderful it is that nobody need wait a single moment before starting to improve the world."

During my time away from my students, I devoted all of my time to Classes 4 Classes. It was my way of doing something to help improve the world. I couldn't just wait for things to happen. Because one of the most profound lessons I learned from Sandy Hook is that the next moment can sweep you away.

I was born with extra empathy. When someone is suffering, I feel it. When someone hurts, I hurt, too. When someone has a need, I want to help fulfill it. I remember as a child going to New York City and walking by homeless people and wanting to do something to make each of their lives better. The feeling didn't pass when I did. It stayed with me long after I got home. Sometimes for weeks afterward I'd lay awake in my comfortable bed, wondering why they didn't have the same comforts that others did, worrying about whether they had dinner or a place to sleep that night. Empathy drove me. I think that's why all of my students were so connected to me. They felt how much I cared, and knew that I'd do anything I could to help them, which is why, after the tragedy, I'd fought so hard for their protection and their peace of mind.

For me, doing for others is organic. It's in my DNA. It's what gets me out of bed in the morning and gives my life meaning. Growing up, my parents emphasized the importance of caring about others, of getting to know people, listening to their stories, understanding their dreams and their heartaches. My dad, who was always helping someone, modeled for me that you do by doing for someone else.

Without my classroom to go to, I needed to find a new place to direct my energies, to fulfill my purpose, to give, and Classes 4 Classes seemed like a natural fit. In just three months, our team had been able to develop the concept into a trial website with working parts. I saw it as the perfect companion to the social curriculums that most elementary schools encourage, and I knew teachers would embrace it as a significant aid in administering those social curriculums into their academically packed programs, which was always a challenge.

Teaching students a social curriculum is making sure they are socially aware. Aware of what connects us and what makes us unique and being accepting of both. Understanding when someone is happy or proud, or sad or upset, and knowing the appropriate response to each. It is about teaching children practical lessons. For instance, if they see another child playing alone on the playground, being able to empathize enough to go up to that child and ask, "Hey! Would you like to play with me?"

The social curriculum I followed was a version of what is called Responsive Classroom, which is based on the premise that children learn best when they have academic as well as solid social and emotional skills. I took training in Responsive Classroom practices and I know how fundamentally important it was in turning out well-rounded students.

———

The problem most teachers face is finding the time and the means to incorporate social lessons into rigorous academic schedules. Finding innovative ways to educate children how to be good people, as well as academically informed, takes tremendous imagination and commitment from a teacher.

In the model I used, each day began with the morning meeting, those few minutes each day that kicked off with the song "Oh, What a Beautiful Mornin'," after which my students hurry to complete their morning work, then gather in the meeting area, where we would sit together (crisscross applesauce, hands in a bowl) to greet one another, share stories, and discuss what the day would bring. The morning meeting helped to establish an environment where everyone felt connected and treated one another with respect and kindness. That sense of camaraderie set the tone for the rest of the day.

A second component was teaching my first-graders how to properly communicate with one another: How do we politely say "Good morning"? What is the appropriate tone to take if someone is upset? What words do you use when someone has hurt your feelings?

The last piece was setting up a support system. I was the central support figure, intervening when students didn't see eye to eye, or scaffolding a lesson for those who were struggling, but the students were also expected to support one another. If they saw a friend making a bad choice, for instance, they were encouraged to remind that friend of what a better choice might be. If they saw one child hurting another, their job was to inform the teacher about what was happening.

Teaching social skills is like any other aspect of getting children to learn. On the early elementary school level, students need repeated exposure to the subject matter before they are able to grasp it, whether the subject is English or empathy. It may seem basic, but someone has to teach us our ABCs before we can learn to read and write, and we have to learn to count to twenty before we can graduate to mathematics. It's no different when teaching children good social skills. They need to learn the nuts and bolts of being socially skilled. For instance, how to be kind, how to share, how to be a good friend. They learn by doing, and that doesn't happen overnight.

The challenge for elementary school teachers is being able to incorporate those kinds of lessons into a seven-hour school day, while still teaching the required eight academic courses. It's a daunting proposition, and one that many educators find frustrating and nearly impossible to pull off. And the problem always is, even when you do manage to fit in social instruction, how can you be sure that telling children how to be kind and caring has resonated with them? You really can't. I was always looking for practical ways for my students to experience those lessons, rather than just take them from me. Classes 4 Classes was a way to do that.

The best tangible evidence I saw of a social curriculum really working was the glow on my students' faces when they helped the class from Tennessee get the whiteboard. They had really embraced the meaning of being kind and charitable. Through that simple exercise, they really got what it felt like to give without expecting anything in return, and it felt good. They learned about kindness and empathy, caring not by simply talking about it but by living it. Even after being faced with such a terrible tragedy, they had chosen love. I couldn't imagine a more valuable life lesson. That small gesture of one class helping another was a step toward making the world a better place. My students were the best example of such valuable lessons. Giving always makes us feel better. Action inspires. And now I had a way (and plenty of time!) to share those lessons with a much larger audience.

Classes 4 Classes would live on a website, which meant its reach was endless. It was an accessible social networking tool with the ability to connect classrooms across the country to care for one another. I knew it would resonate with teachers and their kids. Who wouldn't want to take part in such an optimistic and life-affirming project? I was certain that if I could just get the word out, the response would be the beginning of a movement.

I sat down and composed an initial letter to teachers:

The mission of Classes 4 Classes is to teach every child in our nation to care for another by caring for others, to have genuine interest in the well-being of others, by showing interest. We will cultivate a message that our lives are not separate but, in fact, completely connected. We will create an environment where our students learn to care for others, not by talking about it, but by doing. Students will learn to love by being loving.

Classes 4 Classes is a true example of good. It will help our youngest students to learn the most fundamental lesson: that it is always better to give than to receive. That you can always help someone else. That working together toward a common goal builds a sense of teamwork, community, where everyone is included and actively engaged. Ultimately that as a class they are "sponsoring" another class, giving to that class with no expectation to get anything in return, other than knowing how it feels to give freely.

Anything you can do in your own classrooms in

*association with this project would be awesome! It truly
is all about teaching kids to care. By teaching kindness,
compassion, love and empathy, there is no room for hate.*

The response was immediate and encouraging. Within
weeks we had thirty classrooms, most in Connecticut, but
also schools in Arizona, Texas, New York, Massachusetts,
and New Hampshire wanted to participate.

A fourth-grade class from Connecticut sponsored a sixth-
grade class in New York City and asked the class to write
letters with their "wish lists." "We brainstormed a list of
items we needed or wanted for our classroom," the New
York City teacher wrote. "When one student suggested com-
puters, another student raised his hand and asked if that
was too selfish or too much for someone to get us." Some
requested new desks or new chairs, but most requested
books. "This ESL (English as a second language) class absolutely loves reading and goes through books like I have
never seen before," the teacher wrote. "They often ask to go
into the eighth-grade classroom to look for books they
haven't read before. The thought of having a complete library with new books thrills them." One student wrote
something along the lines of, "We could use books. They are
the key to education and knowledge." The Connecticut class
read all of the letters and voted unanimously to fund a new

classroom library for New York City six-graders. They had already begun raising money.

Two fourth-grade classes, both of them taught by friends of mine, chose to work together to help two classrooms in other states, one that asked for Kindles and the other iPads. The most remarkable thing happened. Once the students got into it, they approached their teachers to say they didn't want to wait for donations to come in to the website to get their projects funded. They wanted to be able to provide the requests of their out-of-state fellow students sooner. "We need to do more," they said. "We want to do more. What can we do to help raise the money?" After a couple of idea sessions, their project got even bigger. They were able to recruit other classes for a giant fourth-grade tag sale. The objective was that every fourth-grader in the school would bring in at least one item they no longer needed to sell at the sale. But the team effort didn't stop there. They also planned a Friday movie night in their school gymnasium for the whole school to attend and planned to solicit donations of juice boxes and popcorn to sell.

Hearing about the initial responses of students was so inspiring. The concept was already working and we hadn't even officially launched the website. *This is what it's all about,* I thought. *Instilling in students how good it feels to be good and caring people by helping one another.* The children wanted to help, wanted to make a difference, they simply needed to be given the opportunity to do it. "How far that little candle throws his beams! So shines a good deed in a weary world," William Shakespeare wrote in *The Merchant of Venice*. Those few good deeds by a handful of schoolchildren would light the way for schoolchildren across the country. I was sure of it.

The website debuted with plenty of fanfare, with a segment on *World News Tonight*. On the night the broadcast aired, my board members and I met at one of the member's homes to watch. The *World News Tonight* piece featured a prerecorded interview they had done with me earlier that week where I talked about the gifts to my class, and our class in Tennessee, and how that exchange had evolved into my new mission, which was Classes 4 Classes. There was a moment, just as the interview was ending, when I talked about how the shooting had changed me. I said that I learned to be grateful for things I had once taken for granted. "You know, it's interesting; the morning of the tragedy I took a picture of the sunrise, which is ironic now, looking back, because that could have been my last sunrise, very easily, so now I try to really enjoy each and every moment. Because you just don't know."

After the broadcast, we launched the site and watched it go live. Donations were already coming in. My eyes teared up with gratitude, for the moment, for all of the support we'd gotten, for the commitment from my fellow board members. But most of all, gratitude for the chance to make a difference. I looked at the faces of the rest of the board and knew from their expression that they were feeling what I was. We had done well.

In our own small way, we were starting to change the world.

Action Is Healing

There is no moving on from what happened at Sandy Hook, but I choose to move forward. For myself. For the people I love and care for. For the community, and the chance to do something meaningful with whatever time I have on this earth. I was raised to believe that each and every one of us who have been given the gift of this precious life has an obligation to give back. Like everyone else, I sometimes immersed myself in the minutia of everyday living and forgot about my larger purpose, but not after what happened at our school. When you witness such a random act of unthinkable brutality, when you are forced to face the painful truth that even innocent children pass away, when you come so close to death that you can feel its breath on your face, it's like the fog lifting to reveal the morning sun.

You see the bigger picture and there's no turning away. You live knowing there isn't time to waste. We need to give our gifts now because no one is guaranteed a tomorrow.

Giving of oneself is the meaning of life, that's what I believe. That's what we're here for. It may not always seem like it, but we're all in this life together and even the small acts of kindness make a difference. Imagine if we took the time that we do, say, gossiping, or shopping, or worrying what others think about us, and used that energy to contribute something positive to humanity. If we don't do something outside of ourselves, beyond ourselves, for others, then what do our lives mean? What mark do we leave on this earth? That was one of the most profound lessons I took from Sandy Hook. I didn't want my legacy to be Kaitlin Roig-DeBellis, survivor of the deadliest mass shooting at a high school or grade school in U.S. history. I wanted it to be Kaitlin Roig-DeBellis, a regular person who surmounted great tragedy by helping to make the world a better place.

I have a giving nature. I think most of us do. But for a long time, I worried that my immense grief would be the obstacle I just couldn't hurdle, the thing that would prevent me from salvaging any kind of a purposeful life. For weeks, I'd lost myself in the intense feelings of sorrow and anger and fear we all felt after the massacre, and that rendered me helpless to see beyond myself. Only after I finally realized that I could make a decision to either be swallowed up by the tragedy or make the hard choice to move forward by channeling that negativity into positive action did I begin to get my life back. That was a powerful feeling, to really understand I had a choice. That as long as I had breath, I had the power to think the thoughts I wanted to think, to do the good I wanted to do, to avenge the destruction wrought by the killer by making sure I lived the meaningful life I was meant to live.

Classes 4 Classes had given me renewed purpose and set me on a positive path. My responsibility was to keep the gathering momentum growing. You can move mountains with a mighty heart, and as fragile as I still sometimes felt, my heart beat strong. Sometimes it felt like my steps were slogging through mud, but whenever they felt heavy and I was tempted to stop pushing ahead, I reminded myself that my mission was bigger than I am and I had a responsibility to others to carry through with what I had started.

Sometimes, to keep myself going, I repeated the wise words of my therapist: "Action is healing." With those words to guide me, I took up challenges and accepted undertakings that I once couldn't have even imagined.

The *World News Tonight* piece got a lot of attention, and, as the founder of the nonprofit, I was receiving accolades. After the show aired, I was contacted by different organizations that wanted to showcase Classes 4 Classes by honoring me.

L'Oréal Paris selected me as a Woman of Worth, one of 10 Inspiring Women Making Beautiful Differences in their Communities. The Chicago International Conference on Education flew me to the annual convention to accept their Dedicated Teacher Award. *Glamour* magazine named me as one of its 2013 Women of the Year, alongside Malala Yousafzai, the brave young Pakistani woman who was shot in the head by the Taliban for fighting for the rights of girls to have an education, and Barbra Streisand, my mom's entertainment idol. I was thrilled to be able to introduce them at the awards ceremony in New York.

The *Glamour* gathering was especially moving for me. Standing on the stage with so many incredible women was humbling to say the least. Arianna Huffington introduced my award, and she made it personal. "As a mother, I'm particularly honored to be presenting this next award," she said. She then spoke briefly about Classes 4 Classes and the importance of its mission to teach children love and compassion and the importance of giving back. I was so grateful for the kind words, but the best part of the evening for me came next when, to my complete surprise, nine of the moms of my first-graders came out onstage. I could hardly believe it. Those wonderful women had taken the time to be there for me. I have never felt so honored, before or since. One stepped up to the lectern to address me for the group. "Kaitlin, what you have done for our families is immeasurable," she said. "We're so proud of everything you have done for our community and how you continue to guide children and inspire the nation with Classes 4 Classes."

I was so touched I could barely speak, but I choked out a few words of appreciation. "This award, like everything I have done this past eleven months, is not for me," I said. "This award is in honor of the twenty-six angels who I know are looking down on us right now. This is for them. I thank you all for honoring me so that I can continue to honor them."

I don't think there was a dry eye in the house. Looking out into the audience, I realized the true magnitude of the impact that Sandy Hook had, not just in our community, but with people everywhere, and from all walks of life. I felt a real collective heartbreak in that room, a genuine mourning for my six colleagues and the twenty first-graders who lost their lives. And I was grateful for the opportunity to remember them in such a public setting.

CHOOSING
HOPE

"Hope is being able to see that there is light despite all of the darkness."

—DESMOND TUTU

Do It Anyway

The praise I was receiving for Classes 4 Classes was wonderful, and I appreciated every kind word. But with all the goodness came criticism, and more lessons. I learned the hard way (doesn't everyone?) that even when you're working from your purest heart, people will pass harsh judgment on you. As much as it hurts, you can't let it stop you from pursuing the things you believe in, or sticking to your core values, or telling your truth, because integrity is the basis of all of the good in the world.

I heard about the rumors started by people I'd never even met, the gist of which was that I'd abandoned my students and run off to take advantage of a tragedy by promoting myself. Nothing could have been further from the truth.

The most hurtful disparagement came from a school acquaintance with whom I had shared a warm relationship prior to the shootings. She'd sent me a message through Facebook telling me that she would no longer be in contact with me. "I can't interact with you anymore," she wrote. "It's too painful to see you walk red carpets when I'm walking the hall in our school." I interpreted what she was saying as, "You abandoned us and I'm still here, so I don't want to see what you're doing now." Her words cut me to the quick.

Did she have any notion of how much I'd wanted to be back at school, or how hard I'd fought to be there? Did she know that I had taken a different path because my return to school had been made impossible? Did she not understand that I would have given anything not to be in the position that led me to my new path? That I would have given everything to turn back the clock to December 13 and somehow be able to save the people who died and spare my students their trauma?

I responded to her by reciting my version of the Golden Rule. "If you don't have anything nice to say, then don't say anything at all." Do unto others as you would have them do unto you. We practiced it every day in the first grade, but as adults it seems that we often forget how hurtful our words and actions can be. I wished my colleague would have thought about the implications of what she wrote before she'd sent the message. Walking the red carpet was not something

I'd sought. I hadn't asked to be on this new path, and I would have given up everything to return to the one I was on until December 14, 2012. I was doing the best I could just to live my life with purpose. I wasn't particularly comfortable in the situations where I was being honored, but as the founder of Classes 4 Classes, as the face of it, I was grateful for the opportunities to bring attention to such an important cause. I wondered how that woman would have felt had someone written such hurtful words to her? In my response to her, I asked that she please consider the pain her words had caused, but she never received my message because she'd unfriended me on Facebook before I got the chance to send it.

One evening, still feeling the sting of the woman's unkind words, I sat down at my computer and searched the names of some people who I believed to be above reproach, role models, to see if even they had suffered from the harsh judgments of others. What I learned is that even Mother Teresa had critics. Reading that caused me to step back and realize that no one, not even the most selfless among us, pleases everyone. What's the saying? You can be the biggest, ripest, juiciest peach, but some people just don't like peaches?

That same night, I came across a poem titled "Do It Anyway." Sometimes it's attributed to Mother Teresa but it was actually written by Kent M. Keith and the verses were posted on a wall at Mother Teresa's home for children in Calcutta. The words had a powerful impact on me.

People are illogical, unreasonable and self-centered. Love them anyway.

If you do good, people will accuse you of selfish, ulterior motives. Do good anyway.

If you are successful, you will win false friends and true enemies. Succeed anyway.

The good you do today will be forgotten tomorrow. Do good anyway.

Honesty and frankness will make you vulnerable. Be honest and frank anyway.

The biggest men and women with the biggest ideas can be shot down by the smallest men and women with the smallest minds. Think big anyway.

People favor underdogs but follow only top dogs. Fight for a few underdogs anyway.

What you spend years building may be destroyed overnight. Build anyway.

People really need help but may attack you if you do help them. Help people anyway.

Give the world the best you have, and you'll get kicked in the teeth. Give the world the best you have anyway.

When the critics came out (and, thank goodness, they were few and far between) I remembered those words. I had started something important and I couldn't let a few critics crush my spirit. I had to do what I knew was right. That doesn't mean the criticism didn't hurt. It did. I was born a people-pleaser and maybe once I would have been frightened away from my mission by people's unkind judgments, or maybe I would have tried to convince them that my intentions were good. But not now. I didn't need to prove my good character; there was no time for that. I just needed to live it.

I began every morning reading that inspiring poem and decided that, going forward, it would be part of my message. I had never spoken in front of a large audience, but I decided to "Do It Anyway" when I was invited to address a group of educators in the Pittsburgh suburb of Seneca Valley on their Back to School day in 2013. I was a bundle of nerves in anticipation of my public speaking debut, but not so much because it was new to me, or because of the size of the crowd. My jitters were about making sure I got my message across. I didn't want to be misunderstood, the way I had been by my former colleague. Yes, I would talk about what my students and I experienced together on the day of the killings, but that wasn't the purpose of my speech and I wanted to make sure that was crystal clear. I'd spent weeks writing and revising my remarks to make sure the meaning of what I intended was what came across, that we cannot control what happens to us in life, only how we choose to react to it. And we can always choose hope.

More than a thousand employees from the district turned out in the school auditorium. My hands shook as I began to speak.

"I am here with you today to share my story," I said. "My story as a teacher, a learner, a leader, a survivor. I share it with you, because I think it may make a difference in how you view each moment, each minute, each day when you are truly aware that life can change in an instant. I share it with you because as educators we have a common bond: to help children."

Much later in my talk, I spoke of the tragedy.

". . . On the morning of December fourteenth, 2012, inside the walls of Sandy Hook Elementary, our school endured a tragedy beyond comprehension. Twenty-six lives were taken far too soon, senselessly and brutally. In the midst of such unimaginable loss, loss that could have very well been the loss of my own life, I had to find meaning again. I could not continue to live the way I had, of thinking I had all of the answers, because now I knew that I did not. Something had shifted inside of me. From that day forward I had to look within, I had to reflect back and I had to look to the future. In life things happen to us, good, bad, and everything in between. I know now that it is not the moment that defines us, but in how we choose to react to the moment."

As I began to tell the story my voice faltered and I wasn't sure if I would be able to continue. But a voice in my head told me to "do it anyway" and I pressed on. "I could start by sharing with you my experience on December fourteenth around nine-thirty in the morning, but my story begins far before that," I said. "So I must start with what is at the core of this: wanting to become a teacher, the journey that brought me there and all of the important lessons that I learned along the way."

I looked out at the audience and saw a sea of compassionate faces, and it gave me strength. These were teachers. My people. I should have known—they understood before I even began to explain. "We each define our purpose when we answer these questions: Who are we? What are our desires, our goals, our ambitions? What is it that we want to do? December 14 is why you know my name, but it tells you nothing about what defines me as a teacher. There are days when our job as a teacher causes us to go far beyond our call of duty . . ." I continued.

After the story about what happened in our classroom that awful day, many in the audience were crying. It was enough of that. I cleared my throat and continued. "The possibility that your life can change in an instant is always possible. Sometimes fortuitously so and others not. Avoiding a head-on collision because you just switched lanes, leaving your home minutes before it burns to the ground, a miraculous healing after suffering a long illness. But then the change can also be for the worse. Your car being side swiped on the highway, a loved one drowning, an angry man entering a school with a semi-automatic weapon intending to take the lives of as many innocent people as possible. Knowing this, there are two things to take away. One, you must live your life in a way so that, if it were your last moment, you would feel good about the choices and decisions in life that you made. Second, you are the one who has the power to choose how you react to these situations. You can react with anger, resentment, or hate, or you can react with love, compassion, empathy, and hope. That choice will define your life going forward."

My students and I were living proof of that. I went on to tell the audience about our classroom project and how helping the class in Tennessee had provided so much joy for my first-graders. "I was reminded on that day that children are able to understand the importance of helping others, of giving, and of making a difference, even after such a tragic situation," I said. "I thought: If, after such a horrific event, we are going to choose: love, consideration, compassion, empathy, hope—which I so believed we should—then we, as teachers, need to teach that to our students and this was a way to teach them. We need our students to have the opportunity to be a part of something that exhibits all of these things, to be a part of something bigger than themselves, bigger than all of us."

Our class was the first class to reach out to another class and say, "What do you need? How can we help you?" My students were able to experience, firsthand, that giving and making a difference in someone else's life is the way to enact positive change. It was our way to give back, after all we had been given. This is where the idea for the nonprofit organization I started was born."

My hour-long speech seemed to go by in a flash and afterward a line snaked around the auditorium. Teachers and administrators and aides and janitors all waited to speak with me. I must have shaken a hundred hands when a woman walked up and said her friend, who was also a teacher in the school, had been diagnosed with cancer earlier that week and was feeling hopeless, but listening to my story, that had changed.

The friend, a lovely woman, middle-aged, was a few people back in the line, and when she reached me I saw a glimmer in her eyes. "I'm going through a very tough time right now," she said. "Earlier this week I got some awful news. I want to thank you for being here and I'm so grateful for having heard your message." She realized, she said, that she had the power to change the way she was looking at her diagnosis and that, rather than focusing on something she had no control over, she was going to focus on what she could do.

Speaking with that woman had a profound impact on me. I had taken a huge leap of faith when I accepted that speaking engagement. I had walked onto that stage with such trepidation, so unsure of my decision to put myself out there, and wondering, *Is what I say going to make a difference? Will it change someone's life for the better?* Because that was the only reason I agreed to be there. My moment with that beautiful woman reaffirmed for me that sharing my story, which was so hard for me to tell, was the right thing to do. She had heard my message in exactly the spirit in which it had been given, and it helped her to change course in her own journey. She had chosen hope, and I was certain that I was exactly where I was supposed to be.

And that had been my prayer.

A Beautiful New Sunrise

When I was growing up, my dad and I would often head down to the reservoir after dinner to feed the geese or the ducks or the fish. It was our special time together and I always looked forward to it. Sometimes we'd just walk along the water's edge looking for rocks to collect. When we found a good one, Dad would always say, "Katie, we found a keeper!" *Keeper* became our way of referring to anything special.

My fiancé, Nick, fit into that category. This is the kind of guy he is: In 2009, on our second date, I'd been telling him about how I had been looking, so far in vain, for a special bell I could use as a gentle reminder for my students when things got a little too spirited in the classroom, the type of bell you tap and it rings once, like the bell in a short-order kitchen that signals when an order is ready. I couldn't find one anywhere. Our next date was the night before the school year began and, when I got into Nick's car, he handed me a gift. As I carefully unwrapped it, I was filled with anticipation, but I never, not in a million years, would have guessed it would be the bell I couldn't find. How thoughtful he was. I had known him a week and he'd taken it upon himself to find what I hadn't been able to after weeks of searching. Five years of being together as of this writing, and he is still just as considerate and kind.

Through all of the tumult after the tragedy, the ups and the downs, the good days and bad days, the dark and the light, the one thing that remained constant was Nick. I couldn't imagine life without him. Nick was a keeper.

We married on August 16, 2013, eight months after that tragic morning at Sandy Hook. Most of the arrangements had been made prior to that day, but the last-minute details had provided a welcome distraction from an otherwise emotionally draining year.

My mom and I left suburban Connecticut three days ahead of the wedding, stopping first in Manhattan to pick up my dress, then heading east to Westhampton to oversee the final preparations for the celebration. Those mother-daughter memories from those few days together are something I will always treasure. The special dinners, the long walks on the beach, the final meetings with the florist and the caterer and the hotel manager to make sure that everything was just right. During those days, I couldn't help but think about how different things might have been. I'm sure my mom was having the same thoughts of gratitude.

Nick and my dad arrived on that Thursday afternoon, followed by a steady stream of friends and loved ones who traveled to Long Island from all over the country. In a matter of hours, our beach day grew from five to twenty-five chairs in the sand, and the expressions of love from our company was as soothing as the summer sun. I could hardly wait for Friday to be able to say "I do" to a lifetime of support, nurturing, friendship, and love.

The wedding day dawned with a huge red sun on a canvas of blue sky. It was a perfect eighty degrees. Shortly after I awoke, my maid of honor delivered a card from Nick. "He wanted you to have this before makeup," she said.

The four-page handwritten letter began:

Tuesday, August 18, 2009, my life changed the moment you walked through the door. I remember going home that night thinking I had met the most beautiful girl. I remember getting butterflies in my stomach, a feeling I never felt before.

. . . As you know, August 28 [the date his mom passed

away] is always a hard day for me, but not that year. At
the cemetery, for the first time ever I remember actually
laughing and talking to my mom, telling her I knew it
was way too soon, but that I thought you might be a
keeper and to please help me to make this work. And from
that day forward we started our journey. I never thought
I would love someone as much as I love you, but I know
someone was looking out for me.

. . . This past year has had many ups and downs. I
know that no matter what life throws at us we will get
through it together. With everything that has happened,
you have showed me you are strong, caring, and an
amazing person, and I am so lucky to have you in my life.
You have made me so proud and humble to be with you.

. . . You are my best friend, my soul mate, my
confidant . . . I can't believe our day is finally here.

Nick once again surprised and surpassed my highest expectations with the letter. It was the most beautiful sentiment from the most beautiful man. I sat on the bed choking
back tears, but it was no use. *Good thing I read this before*
makeup, I thought, as I tucked the letter back in the envelope. How well he knew me.

I spent the next few hours with my mom and the bridal

party, sharing bagels and mimosas, while having our hair and makeup done. I'd read about wedding jitters, but I didn't have a hint of any. I couldn't wait to walk down the aisle to begin my future as Kaitlin Roig-DeBellis.

There was a bittersweet moment, just before my dad walked me down the aisle. He adored Nick, loved him for loving me, but he was losing his daughter and I could see the emotion on his face. Standing there, waiting for the music to begin, my mind wandered back to a conversation I had with my mom, years before. It was after I had suffered a particularly difficult breakup and Mom tried to comfort me by saying that it just wasn't meant to be, there were better things ahead for me. When my spirits still weren't lifted, she added, "All your father and I have ever wanted, and especially your father, is for you to be treasured, to be treated the way you are meant to be." Something changed for me that day, knowing that my dad was aware I was selling myself short and deserved better. I decided, at that moment, that I wouldn't settle for anything less than being treasured. Nick did treasure me, treasure us, and my dad knew that. He respected and admired Nick. In fact, he was so comfortable with who I was marrying that, just as we began our march down the boardwalk to the beach, he joked to me, "You're Nick's problem now, Katie." We both laughed. Dad was grateful that I had found someone who loved me as much as he and my mom did.

As the music played and Dad and I crossed over the dunes on our long walk down to the ocean, I looked out over the water. It was calm and sparkling with the reflection of the sun. *At this moment, life is truly good,* I thought to myself, *and I am going to cherish every second of it. Because who knows what the next moment will bring.*

Nick greeted me with the biggest smile. He was standing with his godfather, who had gotten ordained to be able to marry us and written a personalized wedding script just for us.

"Kaitlin and Nicolas, this day is the culmination of all the dreams and hopes you two have been planning for a very long time," he said, his face beaming. "This is truly the beginning of the new vision of your life together. You have not come to this day without much thought and much anticipation as to what the future holds for you." And then a special word for Nick. "I am sure that today your mother, Lynn, is looking down and celebrating right along with us." How I wish I could have known her, but I knew she had to have been so special to raise such a kind and loving son.

Then it was time to take our vows.

Nick was more comfortable reciting traditional vows,

having recited his most intimate thoughts in his letter to me, but I had decided to write my own.

One thousand four hundred and sixty days: That is how long I have known you. That is when you came into my life and from that day on my life has never been the same. It is now complete.

. . . You have brought light and love to my life. I needed a ride and you picked me up. I needed a bell and you searched one out, found one and bought it for me. You told me you loved me, and I knew I loved you too (I'm sorry I waited a month to tell you).

. . . Life happens. Sometimes we get so caught up in it, it's easy to lose sight of what's truly important. My hope for us is that we will always hold our love at the center of everything we do. That we will wake up every morning and cherish it. That every minute, moment, hour, we will live our lives in a way that honors one another and every person that has gotten us here today. Because in the end it's as much about our friends and family as it is about us.

You are my light when it is dark. You are my rock when I am weak. You are my joy when I am sad. You are my five-year-old when I am feeling way too mature. You are the most amazing man that I have ever met and I thank God every day that you are mine, and that I am yours. Always and forever.

I love you to the moon and I know it's true. And what I want to tell you is . . . I DO!

At that moment, for the first time since a gunman changed my life, and the lives of so many other good and decent people, I felt true happiness.

A few weeks later, a belated wedding gift arrived at my door. Tucked inside was a handwritten note. "Dear Kaitlin and Nicholas," it said. "Sending my congratulations and love on this beautiful new sunrise. Love, Diane Sawyer."

Moving Forward
(Not On)

I had a sign on my desk at school, a paraphrase of a famous Henry Ford quote: "If you think you can, you will," it said. I wanted to be that person who could, but to do that I needed to have faith in myself and in my choices. I realized that the more I put myself out there, the more I would be subjecting myself to that handful of critics who questioned everything from my motives to my character and my genuineness. I needed a thicker skin to flourish. Either that or I would just have to take the arrows in the heart and keep moving forward.

My new mission was never about me. It wasn't about winning awards or soliciting accolades or praise. I would never have sought to have my face on TV or in newspapers or magazines. But I'd chosen to contribute with Classes

4 Classes, and that was about to grow into a larger mission of helping people, by example, to work through their own trials.

I'd chosen hope in the midst of what seemed like a pit of hopelessness and it lifted me out of my despair. I wanted to inspire others to do the same, but to do that I had to share the story of coming back from the darkest moment of my life.

As a teacher, I learned that to bond with my students, I had to be willing to share parts of my life with them that sometimes felt private. Opening myself up created the trust that allowed them to feel safe and speak freely with me. When I accepted that first speaking engagement, the one for the educators near Pittsburgh, I knew I would have to do the same thing. My audience had changed from first-graders to young adults and adults, but, still, for them to feel connected to me and believe in my message, I had to share this very intimate piece of myself. I had to share the story of my adoption, and my path to becoming a teacher and lessons I learned along the way. And the hardest part of all, I had to share what happened on that terrible day in Newtown, the misery of the aftermath, and how I had chosen the new path that had led me to today.

I began my talk this way.

"I'm here with you today to share my story. My story as a

teacher, a learner, a leader, my story as a survivor. I share it with you because I think it will make a difference in how you view each minute, each moment, each day—when you are truly aware that your life can change in an instant. I share it with you because in life we each have a very definite purpose. My purpose has always been to be an educator, to work with, engage, and empower children to be their best selves. We each have goals and ambitions at our core and it is of the utmost importance that we strive to define them, for it is only then that we are able to actively pursue them."

After talking about my early life, my quest to be a teacher, and, finally, the story of what my students and I went through on December 14, 2012, I ended on a hopeful note.

"I am an ordinary person. I am a first-grade teacher. I am just like you. I am someone who, after experiencing the worst tragedy imaginable, made a conscious choice that it wasn't going to define me. I had to choose a path for my own healing. I had to choose to focus on the abundant good that is all around. I had to choose to focus on the positive ways in which I could impact teaching children to care. In your life you will go through hard times, you will have times when you are left searching for answers. You will have times where you feel lost and alone. In the best of times or the worst, I encourage you to always choose hope and to always persevere."

———

After witnessing the effect my story had on others, like the teacher who had just been diagnosed with cancer, I accepted a second invitation to speak, then a third. At every gathering, the same thing happened. When my talk was over, people waited afterward to share their own struggles, and many said they were leaving feeling more hopeful than they'd felt when they came. The more people I came into contact with on those speaking tours, the more certain I was that I was on the right path. Not only was I able to spread the word about Classes 4 Classes, I was able to help people in despair to see that all was not lost. That no matter how bad things seemed, they, like me, could choose hope.

Whenever I doubted myself, or found myself reacting to something negative that was said about me (which I still do sometimes), I called to mind the message I got from the poem by Kent Keith: You can give the world the best you have, and it may never be enough, but give the world the best you have anyway. I had started something important and I couldn't let a few critics crush my spirit. That doesn't mean the criticism didn't hurt. It did. I was born a people-pleaser and maybe once I would have been frightened away from my mission by people's unkind judgments, or maybe I would have tried to convince them that my intentions were good. But not now. I didn't need to prove my good character. There wasn't time for that.

I had a purpose and a responsibility to fulfill it, and I knew my own heart and it was good and kind and genuine. I lived to be a good daughter, a good wife, a good friend, a good teacher, a good person. When someone was down, I did my best to lift them up. When someone was sad, I tried to cheer them. When a stranger smiled at me, I smiled back. I had something to offer and I wanted to give it, so I made the choice to ignore the critics and focus on all of the good around me. Because, in the final analysis, it was never between you and the critics anyway. It is between you and your God. That was one of the best lessons I learned, because it cleared the way for me to take my new path with my head held high and my heart open.

Once I chose to tell my story publicly, my calendar began to fill up. I spoke at commencements, and job fairs, and safety board commissions, and elementary, middle, and high schools and college classes. In San Jose and Amarillo and Hartford and Edmonton and Dallas and Harrisburg and Cleveland.

In every setting, I hit upon the same themes. Purpose. Perspective. Overcoming difficult times. When speaking to educators, I emphasized the value of teachers, and the importance of teaching a social curriculum.

Never let anyone make you forget why you started out on this course. You did it to enrich the lives of children, to make their lives better, to help them succeed. That is all that matters. Meetings and paperwork and high-stakes testing and grading and new initiatives may bog down your days. But it's like anything in life. You have to take the good with the bad. Life is a balance. Focus on those amazing activities and opportunities you have going on in your classroom.

Because I know you do this. You inspire. You excite. You engage. You find ways to make spelling awe-inspiring. You motivate in writing, by sharing your own. You read them literature and take on character voices and make it impossible not to pay attention. You devise cool ways to learn about math and science and geography.

You do all this because you are a teacher. You became a teacher because you knew that your teaching, your lessons, what you put on the board each morning, would make a difference in children's lives.

Early on in my speaking, while I was still getting my feet wet, a school board president in California approached me after one of my talks to say that in all of her years in education she had rarely seen a message that was more effective than the one I had given. "It's powerful and you need to keep sharing it," she said. "I see you as a person who can make significant change." Her affirming words inspired me to keep going.

I spoke to the student body at a high school in Oregon for their Unity Week and was surprised when I walked onstage to see that almost everyone in the audience was wearing the same red and white tees. After I finished speaking, the principal joined me onstage. He thanked me for taking part in their special celebration and sharing my message. Then, he surprised me with a check for Classes 4 Classes. "We decided that since you have helped us in sharing your message, we wanted to help something that we know is important to you. Here is a check for Classes 4 Classes. We wish you all the best in spreading your mission." He brought me to tears when he explained that the red and white shirts I saw in the audience had been purchased by the students for a fundraiser they held to benefit Classes 4 Classes. Those students had a real awareness of unity, of connection, and of working toward the greater good.

Those moments fueled me to continue doing what I was doing. I discovered that I learned something from every encounter, from every story. For every life I touched, someone touched mine. Through the eyes of others, I began to see things I might not have seen before. Appreciate things that maybe once I wouldn't have noticed.

As I sat in an airport waiting for a flight recently, I made eye contact with a man carrying a broom and a dustpan. He smiled at me and I smiled back. The man exuded such warmth and happiness. There was something so special about his energy that I couldn't help but watch him as he worked. I have never seen anyone sweep with such enthusiasm and passion. How easily he could have disliked or resented his work, but instead he embraced it and made the absolute best of it. He appeared to be completely joyful to be doing what he was doing, and he shared his joy by greeting everyone who passed him with a hearty "Good morning!" and a giant smile. Every person, without fail, even those who were rushing for flights, smiled and greeted him back. That man clearly understood that sharing his own happiness went a long way, and he was willing to make the effort to make that difference.

We could all learn a lesson from that gentleman, I thought, as I watched him sweep. Rather than worry about anyone judging him because maybe he didn't have a big corner office or take home a hefty paycheck, he made the most of what he did. He did his job with pride and enjoyment, and in doing so he made his tiny corner of the world a little bit brighter. I'm not sure that before the tragedy, I would even have noticed that man, but now I use him as an example for my own life. I know that my attitude toward my day, my work, my life, determines my own happiness and well-being and affects everyone around me. I try to begin each day, as he did, wearing a smile and greeting everyone I see.

What I took from that lovely man is that whatever you do with your life, whether you sweep, or teach, or run a corporation, you can choose to do it with great joy and, in doing so, make your corner of the world a little bit brighter.

And that is a giant gift to give.

In the two years since Sandy Hook, I have traveled around the country and in Canada sharing my story. I have watched as Classes 4 Classes has grown exponentially and I am filled with hope that we will continue to expand and thrive.

As I look ahead, I am filled with hope for many things. I hope for a healthy and happy life with my husband. I hope to have children of my own. I hope for a long and fulfilling career helping children to learn and grow, and promoting and enabling their success. I hope to keep learning and growing to become the person that I am meant to be.

I know that we will never get answers for Sandy Hook, but I hope to be able to continue to find some light in the darkness that surrounds it. By teaching kindness, compassion, empathy, and love, there is no room for hate.

I have come a long way from the days when I could barely drag myself out of bed or leave my house alone (although I still can't shower with the door closed). I continue to move forward but never on from Sandy Hook. Some days it's one step ahead and two back. But the next day I step forward again.

I still pray, every day, but my prayers have changed from desperate pleas to be delivered from my misery, to prayers of thanks. For every moment, for every hour, for every day. Because nothing is promised.

And now, when I sing "Amazing Grace," it is not to try to quiet my troubled mind, but in gratitude for the wisdom I have taken from that senseless tragedy and the gift of being able to share it with those who are trapped in their own despair. Today I can honestly say, "I once was lost, but now I'm found." I chose hope, and now I see.

EPILOGUE

Since launching Classes 4 Classes in April 2013 we have served more than a thousand students in ten states, and we've been featured in major publications from *People* magazine to *Marie Claire*. Our goal is to get every K–8 public school classroom in the country involved. What better way to triumph over tragedy and honor those we lost at Sandy Hook than to teach kindness?

I have yet to return to the classroom because I want to see my current mission through. And if I ever doubted taking the direction I did, all I need do is read the comments from the children and teachers who have already taken part in Classes 4 Classes. "We may never understand why evil exists, but to know there are people trying to turn bad into good is inspirational," a fourth-grader named Katie wrote.

Epilogue

Our message is resonating with children and I believe it is already making a difference. And, in the words of Mahatma Gandhi "You must be the change you wish to see in our world."

"If you have so much things, you can donate to people that don't have a lot." —*Liam, first-grade student*

"If you do nice things for somebody else—it will grow like a chain reaction!" —*Raven, student*

"One act of kindness really can show a difference in our world. It has to start with someone. Why not us?"
—*Mary Grace, fourth-grade student*

"It's good to help other people because it makes them feel good and it makes us feel good too!"
—*Milo, student*

"We want to do something for another classroom to show that we care for them." —*Karen, student*

"We are giving them kindles because it's nice and we want to show that we care."
—*Hayden, third-grade student*

Epilogue

"It's good to give students kindles because they can read all sorts of texts, like magazines, and learn all sorts of new things." —*MariKate, third-grade student*

"It is wonderful to see how excited our students are to help another class in need."
—*Mrs. Larsen, fifth-grade teacher*

"I hope we get to see the kindergarteners' faces when they get their new projector!"
—*Lauren, fifth-grade student*

"It's good to spread random acts of kindness because you're doing a good thing and helping others and sometimes even helping them achieve their dreams."
—*Colby, fourth-grade student*

"When you do a random act of kindness it makes other people feel good, it's like when u do good it feels good as well." —*Randy, fourth-grade student*

"You get to see the smile on someone's face."
—*Erik, fourth-grade student*

"It makes other people happy, and seeing other people happy makes me want to be more giving. Hopefully

other people will want to make others feel the way they felt when someone did a random act of kindness to them and it will keep spreading."
—*Mena, fourth-grade student*

"I think random acts of kindness are important because there's a lot of wars going on in the world and people are fighting a lot and it feels good to do it too. It helps people who have to see war and fighting not feel sad all of the time." —*Max, fourth-grade student*

"If someone is feeling bad about something, we don't want them to feel hurt so we can prevent that from happening by doing random acts of kindness."
—*Jason, fourth-grade student*

"By paying it forward to this school, you can really show every student that somebody or lots of bodies care about them. That feels great."
—*Kayla, fourth-grade student*

"Being selfless is a theme that everyone should remember and model. Let's walk our talk and start this change of abundant good . . ." —*fifth-grade teacher*

Epilogue

"Boys and girls. Have you ever received a gift from someone for no particular reason?"—*Mrs. Pesce, first-grade teacher* . . . "Yes! My Aunt sewed me a stuffed animal! I loved it, and when I received it I wanted to give her something back to show how happy I was."
—*Grace, first-grade student*

"I hope the class loves the iPad and gets to choose to play with it during indoor recess."
—*Tim, first-grade student*

"Can we make the class a card to send with the gift?"
—*Peyton, first-grade student*

"When you help people, you feel happy inside."
—*Luke, first-grade student*

"When you help someone, you feel proud and good."
—*Kyle, first-grade student*

"When you don't have fun things at school, school isn't fun. I want to help make school fun."
—*Joey, first-grade student*

———

Epilogue

"One good deed can act as a chain reaction. I feel very proud to be helping kindness spread through the nation." —*Matthew, fourth-grade student*

"I think that our small deed can change the world by raising money for a classroom in need of technology and we hope that it will encourage them to sponsor another classroom in need." —*Bella, fourth-grade student*

"I am excited about being in this project to spread kindness around our nation because this will make our world smile. Also, I am proud to know that we are helping schools one by one. Lastly, I think that many people will become happy and will pay it forward." —*Emma, fourth-grade student*

"It's so easy to pass on (pay forward) a good deed." —*Macy, fourth-grade student*

"I have always felt that it is essential that classroom teachers find time in the school day to teach a social curriculum. Teaching students to care for one another is not only the 'right' thing to do in elementary school, it's a necessary life skill and something that I hope my students remember as they grow into adults. My

students and I are thrilled to take part in Classes 4 Classes! We couldn't be more ecstatic to care for another classroom—not just because it is a fun community service activity but because caring for others is our responsibility as human beings."
—*Mrs. Hodge, third-grade teacher*

"I didn't realize how knowledgeable my students were with technology and how strongly they felt about how it helped in their learning. I saw a new light in each of my students when they realized that it was because of them and their thoughtfulness that a classroom would be able to experience a new form of technology and learning. It gave them a sense of power that they didn't realize they had. They felt like they were little people doing something big to help the world. Which I hope is something they carry with them throughout their lives."
—*Mrs. O'Hara, kindergarten teacher*

"Our class needs some books. We don't have enough books. Some of these books aren't even that interesting and when everybody takes them there are not enough books left. We don't even have a full bookshelf."
—*DeAndre, student*

Epilogue

". . . Some books are in terrible condition. When I finally find an interesting book, when I'm on page nine and I flip the page I'm on page seventeen. This is not the only problem. Covers are ripped and the binding is ripped up." —*third-grade student*

"My students are so eager to make a change and help out each other each day and so far we have been compiling at least ten 'Put-Ups,' which are statements that students see or catch someone doing for another person and they write it on a piece of paper. We then read the 'Put-Ups' at the end of each day to reward and applaud nice things that each student does for someone else. I have also made it a point to make sure I say something nice to each one of my students each day and notice that they usually reciprocate the gesture too." —*fifth-grade teacher*

"We may never understand why evil exists, but to know there are people trying to turn bad into good is inspirational." —*fourth-grade student*

When I read each of these as their teachers sent them in, I was reminded just how important our mission was. Reading the last student quote resonated in a way that brought tears to my eyes. I will never have answers to explain the tragedy at our school, but trying to make a positive difference, even a small one, was my way of trying to overcome it.

Today, I end every speech this way:

You can make a difference in our world. What better day to start than today? I encourage you to always know your purpose, follow it, work hard at it, choose to have a positive perspective on how to view the world around you, choose to overcome your own hard times and choose hope within them. Life, in fact, is all about choice and the choice is yours alone to make. Choose hope.

ACKNOWLEDGMENTS

I dedicated this book to the people who helped me through my own darkest hour, and that list is quite lengthy. I would like to pause and take the time now to thank that incredibly important group of people, as I would not be where I am today without them.

I offer my sincerest gratitude to my parents, who, from the day they became mine, have given me their unending love, support, and guidance. To my Nick, thank you for loving me. You are my rock and my "keeper," and it's because of you that I now understand my father's saying.

To my extended family, you have each contributed to my life and in making me the person I am today. I am forever grateful. To Nick's family, thank you for welcoming me into yours. To my best friends (you know who you are), I learned at a very early age that family doesn't have to be blood, and you all are truly my family.

Acknowledgments

To my maternal grandparents, thank you for everything you taught me and for being like parents to me. Your moon hangs in my hallway as a daily reminder of you, not that I could ever forget. To my paternal grandparents, I never had the honor of knowing you, but I know how incredible you both were, because of my dad.

To my birth parents, thank you for giving me up so that I may have had the exact life I was meant to have. I know you knew that all along.

To every teacher I ever had, it is because of you that I became a teacher. I thank you for showing me that we are the difference makers in our world.

To my students, thank you for allowing me to see the world through your first-grade eyes, where everything is new and exciting. I've learned more from each of you than I could ever put into words. Know that you can make all the difference in our world.

To Robin Gaby Fisher, I could have never written this book without you! We make a great team. But you are more than a coauthor, you are now my friend and for that I am very grateful.

To Hannah Brown Gordon, of Foundry Literary & Media, thank you for believing in me and my story and helping me to tell it and share it with others.

To Kerri Kolen and the team at Putnam, I couldn't have asked for a better group to be a part of. You understood the

Acknowledgments

vision for this book from Day One. Thank you for choosing me, so that we can help others to choose hope.

And to the twenty-six angels, there is not a moment or a day that I don't remember you. Your names are the only names that should be remembered:

Charlotte Bacon, 6
Daniel Barden, 7
Rachel Davino, 29
Olivia Rose Engel, 6
Josephine Gay, 7
Ana Grace Marquez-Greene, 6
Dylan Hockley, 6
Dawn Hochsprung, 47
Madeleine F. Hsu, 6
Catherine V. Hubbard, 6
Chase Kowalski, 7
Jesse Lewis, 6
James Mattioli, 6
Grace McDonnell, 7
Anne Marie Murphy, 52
Emilie Parker, 6
Jack Pinto, 6
Noah Pozner, 6
Caroline Previdi, 6

Acknowledgments

Jessica Rekos, 6
Avielle Richman, 6
Lauren Rousseau, 30
Mary Sherlach, 56
Victoria Soto, 27
Benjamin Wheeler, 6
Allison N. Wyatt, 6

ABOUT
CLASSES 4 CLASSES

Classes 4 Classes, Inc. is a 501(c)(3) organization whose mission is to connect classrooms to care and to teach every child in our nation that our lives are not separate but rather completely connected, and that everyone has the power to take action and create positive change. The platform provided by our website actively engages students in learning a social curriculum, not by talking about kindness and empathy but by living it. This encourages the development of their emotional intellect, which is key to forming healthy relationships. Students in one K–8 class give a gift that fulfills a need or educational objective to another K–8 class, anywhere in the country. The receiving classroom is able to accept their gift only after they've selected yet another classroom to give to, thus teaching children to "Pay It 4ward." The author will donate a portion of her proceeds from *Choosing Hope* to her charitable organization Classes 4 Classes. Connect today at www.classes4classes.org.

AFTERWORD

"It's the action, not the fruit of the action, that's important. You have to do the right thing. It may not be in your power, may not be in your time, that there'll be any fruit. But that doesn't mean you stop doing the right thing. You may never know what results come from your action. But if you do nothing, there will be no result."

—Mahatma Gandhi

When I first decided to write *Choosing Hope*, I knew there would be a few who questioned my intentions. I understood I would be criticized for writing about a tragedy still so raw in the hearts and minds of so many. But I couldn't allow the judgments of a few to deter me from turning that life-shattering event into a pursuit of purpose. I believed I had a message worth sharing: a message about how hope buoyed me when I felt as if I was drowning in despair, and one I knew would help others to catch their breath when life had taken it away.

Choosing hope was my life preserver. It was my only control when nothing else was in my control. I couldn't fathom what would make a person murder twenty sweet, innocent children and six good, devoted educators. I couldn't explain why my students and I survived when the shooter ambushed the classrooms nearest us and everyone he encountered in the hallway outside our door. My search for answers to those unanswerable questions was debilitating. Until, one day, perhaps in response to my prayers—or maybe it was my instinct for survival—I looked up at the glittery sunshine and realized that, although my questions would never be answered, and I couldn't turn back time. I had a choice in how I lived my life going forward. I could surrender to the abject sadness that had become my new existence, or I could choose to live with optimism and expectation. So began the first day of the rest of my life. That initial ray of hopefulness turned into a healing process and then a survival guide for the future. "Choose hope" became my mantra, my message, and my purpose.

Very recently, I found myself once again standing at the crossroads of hope and despair. One moment, my husband,

Nick, and I were basking in the joyous news that our prayers of becoming parents had been answered. I was pregnant! We watched the tiny beating heart of our eight-week-old child on an ultrasound machine in awe. A week later, after the same test, I was informed that the heartbeat had faded away.

Nick and I had spent those few splendid weeks planning for a birth. In our rush of blissful anticipation, we picked out names, imagined our baby's first pair of shoes, first set of golf clubs, first trip on an airplane. But the ending we had planned for was not to be. Hearing that my baby had no heartbeat was one of the worst days of my life. But what people forget to tell you is that those worst days don't end with the date on a calendar. The pain of grief and loss endures long after.

In that way, I couldn't help but feel a parallel to the aftermath of my experience on December 14, 2012. Like Sandy Hook, my after was long and hard. It took more than a month to "pass" the baby that had lived inside me; weeks of being poked and prodded to rid my body of something I had so desperately wanted. The sadness overtook me. I couldn't shake it. So I didn't. I allowed myself to feel my sorrow, to let it wash over me and immerse me, to cry until I had no tears left. And, then, I made the conscious decision to, as I always say, move forward, never on. Regrets about what was, or what might have been, live in all of us. They become part of who we are. But when we choose hope, we create a path to who we can be—our best selves.

My book has allowed me to share that intention with thousands of people I would never have otherwise been able to reach: men, women, and children who have read my story of surviving the Sandy Hook massacre, then graciously entrusted me with their own personal narratives of sickness and loss and other misfortunes. In my travels around the country and overseas, I have heard from parents who are grieving the loss of their children, and people living with grave illnesses, and teenagers who were bullied and suffering from depression. One of the most difficult encounters I had was with a young kindergarten teacher whose student died while in her care. One of the most interesting was with a woman who came up to me after one of my talks, visibly shaken. "I just wanted to tell you that I've known for a long time that I need to get out of my unhealthy marriage," she said. "After hearing you speak, I feel empowered. I'm going home today to ask my husband for a divorce."

I've been fortunate to be able to take my message to nearly every state in the country and as far away as Australia and New Zealand, and I've learned many lessons from the people I've met along the way. I know that what happened at our school resonates well beyond Newtown, but until I began traveling with my book I hadn't realized that ours was not only a national tragedy, but also a universal one. People from around the globe have told me that our loss felt like their loss. They cried along with us and prayed for us and grieved our lost loved ones. "I pray for America," a woman in Auckland told me. "When this happened to your country, all of our hearts bled." Even when oceans separate us we are all truly connected.

Every day I receive correspondence from people who have found comfort from *Choosing Hope*. A grieving daughter wrote, "Today marks six months since my dad passed away very suddenly and for me—the person who found him and tried to revive him . . . although our trauma is different, no worse or better, the feelings you describe especially in the aftermath as you tried to rebuild your new life are exactly how I feel. Your book is helping me greatly. I knew from the first quote, 'It's no use going back to yesterday because I was a different person then,' that this was the book for me. . . . I miss my dad every day and I miss the person I used to be, but I am slowly rebuilding and trying to remember that how I respond is up to me, so I thank you for that reminder."

A young mother wrote this: "I have a six-year-old girl about to start the second grade so I was hesitant to read your book. I bought it the other day and read half of it in one sitting (until my daughter wanted my attention!). I have to say that I look at things in a different way already. I notice the good in things more than I did before, and even though we are facing a difficult few months ahead I am reminded of the way you are dealing with what happened to you by choosing hope."

Especially rewarding are the communications I receive from my fellow teachers. I've heard from hundreds of them. "I am a kindergarten/year one teacher and I can relate to your book on so many levels," a teacher from Australia wrote. "Firstly, understanding just how much love we feel in our jobs. Also, my husband was in an accident many years ago where he feared for his life. He experiences panic attacks daily now. They have consumed him at times. Sometimes he is housebound. I'm looking forward to the day he chooses hope too. I know the mind is an incredibly complex and determined thing! We are working on it together."

A first grade teacher from California told me that after twenty-one years of teaching, she had become bored with her job. "We shared the same crazy excitement in the beginning of our careers," she said. "I somewhere recently lost it. With the curriculum standards and demands increasing, I've realized that I've been focused on pleasing my administration and losing focus on my kiddos, thus the excitement to teach. I'm on page 124 of your book and I had to find a way to tell you that I'm grateful to you for writing this, especially since your words brought me back to why I'm in this career. Thank you for writing this book. You've allowed me to move forward in different situations in my life, and given me hope."

A young, aspiring teacher e-mailed, "If you were able to choose hope after what happened, I will always be able to find hope in whatever comes my way."

The love and support from teachers inspired me to get back to the classroom. I am a born educator and I can't imagine doing anything else. I'm presently teaching two college level courses—one for future teachers; the other based on the tenets of *Choosing Hope,* training educators in ways to enable their students to persevere through adversity. The energy I once devoted to my first graders is now spent growing Classes 4 Classes.

One of the greatest gifts to come from the publication of this book has been the attention it has brought to the nonprofit. Our mission, to teach children the power of kindness and compassion through their ability to gift projects to other classrooms and inspire positive change, recently earned us a nod from the Varkey Foundation, which chose us from among 8,500 educators in 150 countries as a finalist for its global teaching prize. IBM has begun working with us to boost our social media presence, and a recent grant from the Kraft Foundation will allow us to create classroom connections throughout New England. We have set our sights on expanding into all fifty states. Robert Kraft, the owner of the New England Patriots, graciously wrote that his family decided to support us because of our message. "I can't think of a more important lesson for children to learn firsthand," he wrote. "Even at a young age, children should be aware that we are all connected and that everyone has the power to take action and help others." I couldn't agree more. If we can teach benevolence to every child there will be no room for hate.

So much has changed since December 14, 2012. The years since Sandy Hook have been transformative. That terrible tragedy put me on a path to a destination unknown at the time, but it has led to a place of real healing. I have met the most generous people in my journey forward and the outpouring of support has been remarkable. They have helped me to find a place of peace in my life, and I have been fortunate to be able to help some of them along the way. The Dali Lama said, "There is a saying in Tibet, 'Tragedy should be utilized as a source of strength.' No matter what sort of difficulties, how painful an experience is, if we lose our hope, that's our real disaster." I feel blessed that I am able to continue spreading my message.

My book has turned out to be exactly what I'd intended.

A healing book. A book that brings people together. A book that promotes kindness, compassion, and empathy.

A book about the power of hope.

I want to take this opportunity to express my heartfelt gratitude to the readers who have found light through the book, and invite new readers to continue to do the same. Especially during these very challenging times, we all need something to hold on to. Something to nourish and sustain us until the sun breaks through the clouds.

In the words of Martin Luther King Jr., "If you lose hope, somehow you lose that vitality that keeps life moving, you lose that courage to be, that quality that helps you go on in spite of it all. And so today I still have a dream."

10/24/16